A Tas... Healthier Choices

Lighter, Lively, Flavorful Recipes

Jacquie Schmit ✕ Eileen Mandryk ✕ Jo Wuth

Three Sisters Publishing Inc.

Front Cover Photograph
Maple-Glazed Salmon Fillets, page 114
Stir-Fried Asparagus and Peas with Sesame Seeds, page 85
Citrus Sprout Salad with Toasted Almonds, page 53

A Taste of Healthier Choices

by
Jacquie Schmit ⊠ Eileen Mandryk ⊠ Jo Wuth

First Printing – September 2005

Copyright © 2005 by
Three Sisters Publishing Inc.
12234 – 49 Street
Edmonton, Alberta   **www.3sistersbooks.com**
Canada T5W 3A8   **E-mail:threesis@3sistersbooks.com**

LIBRARY AND ARCHIVES CANADA CATALOGUING IN PUBLICATION
Schmit, Jacquie

   A taste of healthier choices : lighter, lively, flavorful
   recipes/Jacquie Schmit, Eileen Mandryk, Jo Wuth.

   Includes index.
   ISBN 1-897010-24-9

1. Cookery. 2. Low-fat diet – Recipes.
I. Mandryk, Eileen II. Wuth, Jo,   III. Title.

TX714.S348 2005   641.5'63   C2005-906336-X

Photography by:
Patricia Holdsworth, Patricia Holdsworth Photography,
Regina, Saskatchewan

Page Formatting and Index by Iona Glabus

Designed, Printed and Produced in Canada by:
Centax Books, a Division of PrintWest Communications Ltd.
Publishing Director, Photo Designer & Food Stylist: Margo Embury
1150 Eighth Avenue, Regina, Saskatchewan, Canada S4R 1C9
(306) 525-2304   FAX (306) 757-2439
E-mail: centax@printwest.com   www.centaxbooks.com

Table of Contents

Recipes have been tested in U.S. Standard measurements. Common metric measurements are given as a convenience for those who are more familiar with metric. Recipes have not been tested in metric.

Introduction

This cookbook was born out of necessity. Our family, like many other Canadian families, struggles with an array of medical conditions including diabetes, stroke, heart disease, Crohn's, celiac, lactose intolerance and arthritis. As the family medical problems continued to soar, hosting a family dinner to accommodate everyone's needs became more and more challenging. This prompted our journey into the world of healthier nutrition. This book is the result of many hours of research as well as many hours of testing and trying healthier cooking methods while keeping the flavors we all love.

Nutrition began as a study of what we need to survive in the most basic sense. Today, with advanced technology, new information helps us to better understand the importance of healthier choices in our diets.

We really are what we eat. To have a healthy body, we must fuel it with healthier food choices, nourishing it at the cellular level. Cells are the fundamental units of life – the bricks from which all tissues and organs are made. Our cells are constantly communicating with each other, responding to their environment and to the signals they receive. If our cells cannot operate efficiently, the functioning of our tissues and organs will become compromised and we will experience a diminishment of physical functioning and the onset of a host of health concerns and diseases. So by keeping our cells well nourished, we are keeping ourselves well nourished.

Please remember to follow the Canadian Food Guide, as all food groups are important to your health.

Jacquie Schmit
For We Sisters Three

Breakfasts & Breads

French Toast
Waffles & Pancakes
Scones
Muffins
Breads

Peanut Butter and Banana French Toast Sandwich

Tasty and very filling, this is loved by young and old alike.

1-2 tbsp.	peanut butter	15-30 mL
4	slices whole-grain bread	4
2	bananas	2
2	eggs	2
¼ cup	low-fat milk	60 mL
½ tsp.	vanilla	2 mL
½ tsp.	ground cinnamon	2 mL
¼ tsp.	salt	1 mL

Spread peanut butter over bread slices. Slice each banana lengthwise into 4 pieces; sandwich between bread. In a shallow bowl or pie plate, whisk together eggs, milk, vanilla, cinnamon and salt. Add sandwiches, turning to soak up egg mixture. In a large frying pan, heat oil over medium-high heat; cook sandwiches for about 5 minutes, or until browned on both sides. Serve immediately with Orange Blueberry Sauce or Orange Ginger Sauce (recipes follow).

Serves 2

Orange Blueberry Sauce:

½ cup	sugar	125 mL
1 tbsp.	cornstarch	15 mL
1 cup	cold water	250 mL
1	orange, grated zest and juice of	1
1 cup	fresh blueberries, or frozen, thawed	250 mL

In a small saucepan, combine sugar and cornstarch; blend in water, orange zest and juice and blueberries. Over medium heat, stirring constantly, cook until sauce is thickened and clear, about 3-4 minutes. Serve warm.

Makes 2 cups (500 mL)

Orange Ginger Sauce

Oranges and ginger inspire one another. Serve with pancakes; drizzle over frozen yogurt.

1 cup	unsweetened orange juice	250 mL
2 tbsp.	liquid honey	30 mL
2 tsp.	cornstarch	10 mL
1 tsp.	grated orange zest	5 mL
⅛ tsp.	ground ginger	0.5 mL
1 cup	peeled, chopped orange segments OR 10 oz. (284 mL) can mandarin oranges, drained	

In a small saucepan, combine orange juice, honey, cornstarch, orange zest and ginger; stir to mix well. Cook over medium heat, stirring constantly, until mixture thickens, about 2-3 minutes. Remove from heat, and stir in oranges; set aside to cool. Serve slightly warm or cold. To store, refrigerate in a tightly covered container for up to 3 days.

Makes 1½ cups (375 mL)

Peanut Butter Fruit Spread

An amazing flavor combination. Addictive!

1 cup	peanut butter	250 mL
¼ cup	finely chopped dates OR dried apricots	60 mL
¼ cup	finely chopped dried apple	60 mL
1 tbsp.	liquid honey	15 mL
1 tbsp.	unsweetened orange juice	15 mL
1 tsp.	grated orange zest	5 mL

In a small bowl, combine all ingredients; stir well. Serve on whole-grain toast, biscuits, scones or pancakes. To store, refrigerate in a covered container for up to 1 week.

Makes 1½ cups (375 mL)

Three-Grain Buttermilk Waffles
with Apple Berry Sauce

Even the most sluggish morning appetite will appreciate these wholesome and nutritious waffles. Sauce can be made with seasonal berries or your favorites.

Apple Berry Sauce:

¾ cup	apple cider	175 mL
2	apples, cored, peeled and chopped	2
½ tsp.	vanilla	2 mL
1 cup	fresh raspberries, strawberries and blueberries	250 mL

Three-Grain Waffles:

¼ cup	flaxseeds	60 mL
¼ cup	whole-wheat flour	60 mL
¼ cup	buckwheat flour	60 mL
¼ cup	all-purpose flour	60 mL
2 tsp.	brown sugar	10 mL
2 tsp.	baking powder	10 mL
¼ tsp.	salt	1 mL
2	eggs, separated	2
1 cup	low-fat buttermilk	250 mL

Sauce: Bring apple cider to a boil in a large frying pan over high heat and cook for 1 minute. Reduce heat to medium-low; add apples and simmer until tender-firm, about 4 minutes. Remove from heat and let cool to room temperature. Stir in vanilla and fresh berries.

Waffles: Place flaxseeds in a food processor, and process until the consistency of coarse flour. Transfer to a large bowl and add whole-wheat flour, buckwheat flour, all-purpose flour, brown sugar, baking powder and salt. Stir to mix well. Combine egg yolks and buttermilk in a small bowl. Beat egg whites in a small bowl until stiff peaks form.

Make a well in the center of dry ingredients and stir in yolk mixture. Gently fold in whites. Spray waffle iron with nonstick cooking spray. Preheat iron. Spoon batter into iron, approximately ½ cup (125 mL) per waffle. Cook until golden brown and crisp, about 2 minutes. Repeat with remaining batter. Serve warm with Apple Berry Sauce.

Makes 8 waffles

Pictured on page 17.

Cinnamon Oat Bran Pancakes

These spicy oat bran pancakes will give you a healthful, satisfying start to a busy day. These are wonderful served with a berry sauce, see pages 6 and 8.

¾ cup	oat bran	175 mL
¾ cup	all-purpose flour	175 mL
1 tbsp.	sugar	15 mL
½ tsp.	baking powder	2 mL
½ tsp.	ground cinnamon	2 mL
¼ tsp.	baking soda	1 mL
⅛ tsp.	salt	0.5 mL
2	egg whites, slightly beaten	2
1¼ cups	low-fat buttermilk	300 mL
1 tbsp.	olive oil	15 mL

In a large bowl, combine oat bran, flour, sugar, baking powder, cinnamon, soda and salt. In a small mixing bowl, combine the slightly beaten egg whites, buttermilk and oil; beat with a fork just until combined and add to the dry ingredients, stirring just until combined. Spray a cold, large frying pan or griddle with nonstick spray coating; heat pan over medium heat. Spoon ¼ cup (60 mL) portion of batter onto hot pan. Cook until golden, turning once. Serve immediately with your favorite fruit, jam, syrup or sauce.

Makes 8-10 pancakes

Ginger Oat Pancakes

The pancake batter can be made the night before; it can also be covered and stored in the refrigerator for up to two days.

1½ cups	low-fat milk	375 mL
¾ cup	rolled oats	175 mL
1 cup	all-purpose flour	250 mL
1½ tsp.	baking powder	7 mL
1 tsp.	ground cinnamon	5 mL
½ tsp.	ground ginger	2 mL
¼ tsp.	baking soda	1 mL
¼ tsp.	salt	1 mL
1	egg, beaten	1
3	egg whites, beaten	3
2 tbsp.	olive oil	30 mL
2 tbsp.	molasses	30 mL

In a large saucepan, stirring constantly, heat milk over low heat just until hot. Stir in rolled oats. Remove from heat; let stand 5 minutes. In a large bowl, combine flour, baking powder, cinnamon, ginger, baking soda and salt. In a separate bowl, combine beaten egg, beaten egg whites, olive oil and molasses; stir into oat mixture. Add oat mixture to flour mixture; stirring only until moistened. Pour scant ¼ cup (60 mL) batter onto a hot, lightly buttered heavy frying pan. Cook until golden brown, turning to cook other side when surface is bubbly with slightly dry edges. Serve immediately with fresh fruit or fruit syrup.

Makes 10-12 pancakes

The soluble fiber in rolled oats has been shown to help reduce cholesterol by 8-23 percent. Daily consumption of 1½ cups (375 mL) of cooked oatmeal, 2 oat muffins or 1 cup (250 mL) of cooked oat bran is recommended. You can substitute rolled oats for up to ⅓ of the flour in muffins, cakes, cookies and breads, and also use it to extend the meat in meatloaves and meat balls.

Buttermilk Refrigerator Pancakes

A make-ahead recipe with delicious variations – what could be better.

2 cups	all-purpose flour	500 mL
2½ tsp.	baking powder	12 mL
1 tsp.	baking soda	5 mL
¾ tsp.	salt	3 mL
2 tbsp.	sugar	30 mL
2	eggs, lightly beaten	2
2¼ cups	low-fat buttermilk	550 mL
3 tbsp.	olive oil	45 mL

In a large bowl, combine flour, baking powder, baking soda, salt and sugar; stir well. In a small bowl, combine lightly beaten eggs, buttermilk and oil; add to dry ingredients, stirring just until moistened. If batter is too thick, gradually add water to reach desired consistency. Pour about ¼ cup (60 mL) batter onto a hot griddle. Turn pancakes when tops are covered with bubbles and edges look cooked.

Makes 16 pancakes

Variations:

Blueberry Pancakes: Fold 1 cup (250 mL) fresh blueberries into batter just before cooking. Cook as above. You may also substitute your favorite fruit for the blueberries and cook as above.

Whole-Wheat Pancakes: Substitute 1 cup (250 mL) of whole-wheat flour for all-purpose flour; mix and cook as above.

Note: Pancake batter may be placed in a tightly covered container and stored in the refrigerator for up to 1 week.

Egg Substitutions: 1 egg white and 2 tsp. (10 mL) olive oil can be substituted for 1 whole egg OR for low cholesterol cooking – substitute 2 egg whites for 1 whole egg.

Herbed Buttermilk Biscuits

Warm biscuits with flecks of fresh herbs and crusty Cheddar cheese – irresistible!

1¾ cups	all-purpose flour	425 mL
1 tbsp.	chopped fresh chives	15 mL
1 tbsp.	chopped fresh dill	15 mL
1 tsp.	chopped fresh basil	5 mL
¼ tsp.	baking soda	1 mL
¼ cup	butter OR margarine	60 mL
½ cup	shredded reduced-fat Cheddar cheese, divided	125 mL
¾ cup	low-fat buttermilk	175 mL
1	egg white, lightly beaten	1

Preheat oven to 425°F (220°C). In a large bowl, mix flour, chives, dill, basil and baking soda. Cut in butter with a pastry blender or 2 knives until mixture resembles coarse crumbs. Stir in ¼ cup (60 mL) of the Cheddar cheese. Make a well in the center and pour in buttermilk. Mix with a fork until a soft, sticky dough forms. Drop heaping tbsp. (17 mL) of dough onto ungreased baking sheets, making 18 biscuits. Brush biscuits with egg white and sprinkle with remaining Cheddar cheese. Bake until puffy and golden, 15-20 minutes. Serve warm or wrap well and freeze for up to 3 months.

Makes 18 biscuits

Pictured on page 35.

Whole-Wheat Tea Biscuits

Everyone's favorite is made even better with whole-wheat goodness.

1 cup	all-purpose flour	250 mL
1 cup	whole-wheat flour	250 mL
4 tsp.	baking powder	20 mL
1 tsp.	salt	5 mL
½ cup	butter OR margarine	125 mL
¾ cup	low-fat milk	175 mL

Preheat oven to 425°F (220°C). In a large mixing bowl, combine flours, baking powder and salt. With a pastry blender or 2 knives, cut in butter until mixture resembles coarse crumbs. Add milk all at once, stirring with a fork to make a soft dough. Turn dough out onto lightly floured surface; knead gently about 10 times. Roll out to ½" (1.3 cm) thickness; cut with 2" (5 cm) round cookie cutter. Place biscuits on ungreased baking sheets; bake for 10-15 minutes, or until lightly browned.

Makes 15 biscuits

Tangy Cheddar Cheese Scones

A zesty, nutritious variation of old-fashioned scones. Tasty warm or cold.

1 cup	all-purpose flour	250 mL
⅔ cup	whole-wheat flour	150 mL
¼ cup	oat bran	60 mL
2 tbsp.	sugar	30 mL
2 tsp.	baking powder	10 mL
¾ tsp.	EACH cayenne pepper and salt	3 mL
½ tsp.	baking soda	2 mL
2 tbsp.	olive oil	30 mL
1 tbsp.	Dijon mustard	15 mL
¼ cup	grated fat-reduced Cheddar cheese	60 mL
1 cup	plain low-fat yogurt	250 mL

Preheat oven to 400°F (200°C). In a large bowl, combine flours, oat bran, sugar, baking powder, cayenne, salt and baking soda. With a pastry blender or 2 knives, cut in oil and mustard until mixture is evenly moistened. Stir in cheese. Make a well in center of dry ingredients and stir in yogurt until combined. Do not over-mix. Transfer dough to a lightly buttered baking sheet and, with floured hands, shape into an 8" (20 cm) round. Score circle into eighths, cutting through the dough, but not separating the wedges. Bake for 25-30 minutes, or until golden brown and cooked through. Cool 10 minutes on pan before serving.

Makes 8 scones

Pictured on page 69.

Oat and Orange Scones

Rolled oats add texture, flavor and great fiber to these lovely scones.

1 cup	all-purpose flour	250 mL
3 tbsp.	sugar	45 mL
1½ tsp.	baking powder	7 mL
1 tsp.	grated orange zest	5 mL
⅓ cup	butter OR margarine	75 mL
1 cup	rolled oats	250 mL
2	egg whites, slightly beaten	2
2 tbsp.	unsweetened orange juice	30 mL

Preheat oven to 400°F (200°C). In a large bowl, combine flour, sugar, baking powder and orange zest. With a pastry blender or 2 knives, cut in butter until mixture resembles coarse crumbs. Stir in oats. In a small bowl, combine slightly beaten egg whites and orange juice; stir into dry ingredients. (dough will be sticky). Transfer dough to a lightly floured surface; roll or pat dough into a 7" (18 cm) circle. With a floured knife, cut circle into 12 wedges. Place wedges on a lightly buttered baking sheet. Brush tops with milk. Bake for 12-15 minutes, or until golden brown. Serve warm with your favorite preserves.

Makes 12 scones

Whole Wheat Soda Bread

Warm soda bread is a perfect partner for a bowl of hearty soup. This is very easy to make and delicious.

1¾ cups	all-purpose flour	425 mL
3 cups	whole-wheat flour	750 mL
1½ tsp.	EACH salt and baking soda	7 mL
3 tbsp.	butter OR margarine	45 mL
2 cups	low-fat buttermilk	500 mL

Preheat oven to 400°F (200°C). In a large bowl, combine flours, salt and baking soda. Cut in butter with a pastry blender or 2 knives. Add buttermilk and stir to combine well. Place dough on a lightly floured surface and form into 2 rounds about 2" (5 cm) thick. Place rounds on lightly buttered baking sheets and, with a sharp knife, cut a deep X on top of each round.

Bake for 25-30 minutes, or until lightly browned.

Makes 2 rounds

Blueberry Muffins

These are especially great when blueberries are in season. Wonderful for coffee-time snacks with a serving of fresh fruit.

1	egg white	1
1 tsp.	lemon juice	5 mL
1¾ cups	all-purpose flour	425 mL
3 tsp.	baking powder	15 mL
¼ tsp.	salt	1 mL
3 tbsp.	sugar	45 mL
1 cup	low-fat milk OR skim milk	250 mL
¼ cup	olive oil	60 mL
1 cup	fresh blueberries or frozen, thawed and drained	250 mL

Preheat oven to 400°F (200°C). In a small bowl, beat egg white with lemon juice until stiff; set aside. In a large bowl, combine flour, baking powder, salt and sugar; stir to combine well. Make a well in the dry ingredients; add milk and oil. Stir only until mixture is just combined. Fold beaten egg white into batter. Place blueberries in a colander and rinse under cold water. Drain and fold gently into muffin batter. Fill lightly buttered muffin tins ⅔ full. Bake for 20-25 minutes, or until golden brown. Transfer muffins to a wire rack to cool completely. Store in a tightly covered container in the refrigerator for up to 5 days or wrap well and freeze for up to 3 months.

Makes 12 muffins

Banana and Raisin Bran Muffins

No added sugar – just natural fruit flavors.

4	eggs, lightly beaten	4
2 cups	skim milk	500 mL
¾ cup	frozen apple juice concentrate, thawed	175 mL
1 cup	mashed banana (3-4 bananas)	250 mL
2 tsp.	vanilla	10 mL
1 cup	all-purpose flour	250 mL
1 cup	whole-wheat flour	250 mL
2 cups	bran	500 mL
1½ tsp.	baking powder	7 mL
1 tsp.	baking soda	5 mL
2 tsp.	ground cinnamon	10 mL
1 cup	raisins, washed and dried	250 mL

Preheat oven to 350°F (180°C). In a large bowl, beat eggs lightly; stir in milk, apple juice concentrate, mashed bananas and vanilla. In a separate large bowl, combine all-purpose flour, whole-wheat flour, bran, baking powder, baking soda, cinnamon and raisins; stir well to combine. Make a well in the dry ingredients; add liquid ingredients, stir until just combined. Fill lightly buttered muffins tins ⅔ full. Bake for 25-35 minutes, or until lightly browned. Transfer to a wire rack to cool completely. Store in a tightly covered container in the refrigerator for up to 5 days or wrap well and freeze for up to 3 months.

Makes 24 muffins

Bananas are rich in potassium, which helps to prevent and reduce high blood pressure and protect against atherosclerosis. They are a good fiber, Vitamin C and B6 source. They help to correct elimination problems. Bananas can help your body absorb calcium better and reduce the risk of kidney cancer. One banana a day is the recommended amount.

Breakfasts & Breads

Three-Grain Buttermilk Waffles with Apple Berry Sauce, page 8
Fruits Ahoy, page 142

Fruit and Nut Oat Bran Muffins

Apples and cranberries make these muffins moist and flavorful.

2	apples, peeled and cored	2
1 cup	fresh cranberries or frozen, thawed	250 mL
3 tbsp.	olive oil	45 mL
1¾ cups	low-fat milk	425 mL
1	egg	1
¾ cup	sugar	175 mL
1½ cups	all-purpose flour	375 mL
1 cup	EACH rolled oats and bran	250 mL
2 tsp.	baking powder	10 mL
1 tsp.	baking soda	5 mL
4 tsp.	ground cinnamon	20 mL
½ tsp.	salt	2 mL
1 cup	chopped walnuts	250 mL

Preheat oven to 400°F (200°C). In a covered blender or food processor, combine apples, cranberries, oil, milk, egg and sugar; blend or process until mixture is well combined. In a large bowl, combine flour, rolled oats, bran, baking powder, soda, cinnamon, salt and walnuts; stir well. Make a well in the center and pour in the blender mixture; mix until just combined. Fill lightly buttered muffin tins ⅔ full; bake for 20-25 minutes, or until lightly browned. Transfer to a wire rack to cool completely. Store in a tightly covered container in the refrigerator for up to 5 days or wrap well and freeze for up to 3 months.

Makes 24 muffins

Cinnamon – One of the most-loved and oldest spices, cinnamon has long been used in natural medicine treatments. Recent studies indicate that cinnamon may help to reduce LDL cholesterol, triglycerides and blood sugar. It also has insulin-like properties that may benefit people with Type-2 diabetes. The recommended amount is ½ tsp (2 mL) per day. Don't consume cinnamon with sugar or tea – the benefits are reduced. Try plain yogurt with fresh fruit and sprinkle it with cinnamon or add cinnamon to other foods.

Raisin Bran Muffins

A wholesome, tasty, moist muffin.

¼ cup	butter OR margarine, softened	60 mL
¼ cup	brown sugar	60 mL
¼ cup	molasses	60 mL
2	eggs	2
1 cup	low-fat milk	250 mL
1½ cups	bran	375 mL
1 cup	all-purpose flour	250 mL
1½ tsp.	baking powder	7 mL
½ tsp.	baking soda	2 mL
½ tsp.	salt	2 mL
¾ cup	raisins, washed and dried	175 mL

Preheat oven to 400°F (200°C). In a large bowl, with an electric mixer on medium speed, cream butter and sugar together. Add molasses and eggs and beat until well combined. Stir in milk; add bran and mix until well combined. In a small bowl, combine flour, baking powder, baking soda and salt; stir to combine. Stir flour mixture into bran mixture and combine well. Stir in raisins. Fill lightly buttered muffin tins ⅔ full. Bake for 15-20 minutes. Cool on a wire rack. Store muffins in an air-tight container in the refrigerator for up to 5 days or wrap well and freeze for up to 3 months.

Makes 12 large muffins

Multigrain Bread

In this recipe, unsweetened applesauce is used to activate the yeast instead of sugar. This is a very large recipe that makes 6 loaves at a time.

4 cups	warm water	1 L
2 cups	unsweetened applesauce	500 mL
2 tbsp.	dry yeast	30 mL
10 cups	whole-wheat flour	2.5 L
2 cups	multigrain cereal*	500 mL
1 tbsp.	salt	15 mL
1 tbsp.	ground cinnamon (optional)	15 mL

In a large bowl, stir water, applesauce and yeast together gently. Allow the yeast to foam for about 10-15 minutes. In a separate large bowl, mix together all the dry ingredients; stir well to combine. Add the dry ingredients to the applesauce mixture and mix well. Place dough on a lightly floured surface and knead until it is soft and elastic, about 8-10 minutes. If the dough is too wet, add a little more flour; if too dry, add a little warm water. Place the kneaded dough in a lightly oiled bowl, turning once to oil top. Cover and let rise in a warm place for 30-45 minutes. Punch down dough and form into loaves the size of your choice. Place loaves in lightly oiled pans.

Preheat oven to 350°F (180°C). Allow the formed loaves to rise in a warm place for 1-1½ hours. Bake for 25-35 minutes, or until nicely browned. Remove to wire racks to cool completely. Wrap well and store in the refrigerator for up to 3 days or wrap well and freeze for up to 3 months.

Makes 6 loaves

* *Multigrain cereal can be purchased at health food stores and consists of rolled oats, barley, flax, rye and oat flour. Some commercial brands are Sunny Boy and Red River Cereal.*

Oats, Seeds and Grain Bread

These wholesome round loaves are filled with grains, oats, nuts and seeds.

3-4 cups	all-purpose flour	750 mL-1 L
1 cup	rolled oats, divided	250 mL
¼ cup	sugar	60 mL
3 tbsp.	chopped walnuts	45 mL
2 tbsp.	sunflower kernels	30 mL
2 tsp.	active dry yeast	10 mL
¾ tsp.	salt	3 mL
¾ cup	water	175 mL
⅓ cup	olive oil	75 mL
¼ cup	low-fat buttermilk	60 mL
¼ cup	honey	60 mL
2	eggs, divided	2
¾ cup	whole-wheat flour	175 mL
1 tbsp.	cold water	15 mL

In a mixing bowl, combine 2 cups (500 mL) all-purpose flour, ¾ cup (175 mL) oats, sugar, walnuts, sunflower kernels, yeast and salt. In a small saucepan, combine water, oil, buttermilk and honey; set over medium heat and, stirring constantly, cook until thermometer reaches 120°-130°F (49-54°C). Remove from heat and stir into dry ingredients. With an electric mixer, beat mixture until well blended. Beat in 1 egg until smooth. With a wooden spoon, stir in whole-wheat flour and enough remaining all-purpose flour to form a soft dough. Turn onto a floured surface; knead until smooth and elastic, about 6-8 minutes. Place in a lightly buttered bowl, turning once to butter top. Cover and let rise in a warm place until doubled, about 1 hour. Punch down dough; turn onto a lightly floured surface. Divide in half; shape into round loaves. Sprinkle 2 tbsp. (30 mL) oats on a lightly buttered baking sheet; place loaves over oats. Cover and let rise until doubled, about 45 minutes.

Preheat oven to 350°F (180°C). Beat remaining egg and cold water; brush over loaves. Sprinkle with remaining oats. Bake for 20-25 minutes, or until golden brown. Cool on wire racks. Wrap and store for 2 days or wrap well and freeze for up to 3 months.

Makes 2 loaves

Whole-Wheat and Sesame Seed Bread

The nutty flavor of sesame seeds adds a slightly sweet flavor to this bread. Try the red, brown or black sesame seeds for added color.

2 tbsp.	active dry yeast (2 x 1 tbsp./7 g env.)	30 mL
1 cup	warm water	250 mL
1 cup	warm low-fat milk	250 mL
½ cup	honey	125 mL
3 tbsp.	olive oil	45 mL
1 tbsp.	salt	15 mL
1	egg, lightly beaten	1
¼ cup	sesame seeds, toasted	60 mL
2½ cups	whole-wheat flour	375 mL
3-3½ cups	all-purpose flour, divided	750-825 mL
2 tbsp.	butter OR margarine, melted	30 mL
	sesame seeds for garnish (optional)	

In a mixing bowl, dissolve yeast in water. Add milk, honey, oil, salt, egg, sesame seeds, whole-wheat flour and 1½ cups (35 mL) all-purpose flour. Beat until smooth. Stir in enough remaining all-purpose flour to form a stiff dough. Turn onto a floured surface; knead until smooth and elastic, about 6-8 minutes. Place in a lightly buttered bowl, turning once to butter top. Cover and let rise in a warm place until doubled, about 1 hour. Punch down dough. Turn onto a lightly floured surface; divide in half. Shape into loaves. Place in 2 lightly buttered 3 x 5 x 9" (8 x 13 x 23 cm) pans. Brush with melted butter. Sprinkle with additional sesame seeds if desired. Cover; let rise until doubled, about 45-60 minutes.

Preheat oven to 350°F (180°C). Bake for 35-40 minutes, or until golden. Remove from pans to wire racks to cool. Wrap and store for 2 days or wrap well and freeze for up to 3 months.

Makes 2 loaves

Whole-Wheat and Honey Breadmaker Bread

7½ oz.	water, at room temperature	213 mL
2 cups	whole-wheat flour	500 mL
¼ cup	liquid honey	60 mL
1 tsp.	salt	5 mL
¾ tbsp.	gluten	11 mL
1 tbsp.	butter OR margarine	15 mL
1 tbsp.	dry milk powder	15 mL
1¾-2 tsp.	breadmaker yeast	9-10 mL

Add all ingredients for bread in the order suggested by your bread machine manual. Process on the whole-wheat cycle according to the manufacturer's directions.

Makes 1, 1 lb. (500 g) loaf

Variation: For a lighter bread, use 1 cup (250 mL) white flour and 1 cup (250 mL) whole-wheat flour and reduce gluten by ½ tsp. (2 mL).

Grains – Grains in their natural unrefined state feature a host of important nutrients. The more refined they are, the more they become stripped of their natural goodness. Whole grains are an excellent source of dietary fiber and manganese; as well, most are also a very good source of tryptophan, magnesium, thiamin, phosphorus and selenium.

Health benefits of whole grains include: good for the cardiovascular system – actually lowers the risk of developing high cholesterol and high blood pressure; better blood sugar control; powerful antioxidants that work in multiple ways to prevent disease; high insoluble fiber content speeds intestinal transit time.

Soups

Chilled Fruit
Creamy or Hearty Vegetable
Seafood
Chicken
Beef

Chilled Creamy Melon and Mango Soup

A mild flavored, creamy soup. Very refreshing served on a hot day.

2 cups	cubed cantaloupe	500 mL
1 cup	diced mango	250 mL
¾ cup	unsweetened orange juice	175 mL
½ cup	low-fat plain yogurt	125 mL
2 tbsp.	lime juice	30 mL
2 tbsp.	liquid honey	30 mL

In a food processor or blender, combine cantaloupe and mango; process until smooth. Add orange juice, yogurt, lime juice and honey. Blend or process until well combined. Chill before serving. Soup can be refrigerated for up to 3 days.

Serves 4

Pictured on page 35.

Chilled Melon and Orange Soup

This soup is rich in flavor and power-packed with vitamin C.

1	ripe cantaloupe	1
1 cup	low-fat plain yogurt	250 mL
1	medium orange, juice and grated zest of	1
¼ tsp.	ground cinnamon	1 mL
	fresh mint or orange slices for garnish	

Cut cantaloupe in half; remove seeds; scoop out pulp. In a food processor or blender, purée pulp; add yogurt, orange juice, orange zest and cinnamon; process until well combined. Refrigerate until chilled, about 2-4 hours. Garnish with fresh mint or orange slices.

Serves 4

Chilled Strawberry and Yogurt Soup

This elegant creamy strawberry soup has a surprising hint of cinnamon.

1 cup	unsweetened apple juice	250 mL
1 cup	water, divided	250 mL
⅓ cup	sugar	75 mL
½ tsp.	ground cinnamon	2 mL
2 cups	fresh strawberries	500 mL
2 cups	low-fat strawberry yogurt	500 mL

In a medium saucepan, combine apple juice, ¾ cup (175 mL) water, sugar and cinnamon. Place over medium heat and bring to a boil. Remove from heat; cool. Place strawberries and remaining ¼ cup (60 mL) water in a blender or food processor; cover and process until smooth. Transfer strawberry mixture to a large bowl; add apple juice mixture and yogurt. Cover; refrigerate until well chilled. Garnish with additional strawberries if desired.

Serves 6-8

Variation: For *Chilled Blueberry and Orange Yogurt Soup* substitute fresh blueberries for the strawberries and orange low-fat yogurt for the strawberry yogurt. Garnish with grated orange zest if you wish.

Note: Sweeten soups to your taste. You can substitute liquid honey for the sugar.

The antioxidant, phenol content of strawberries makes them a heart-protective, anti-cancer and anti-inflammatory food. They are an excellent source of Vitamins C, K and manganese, and a very good source of dietary fiber. A daily serving of strawberries (8 berries) has been shown to increase blood folate levels and decrease systolic blood pressure; enhance memory function and help with the management of rheumatoid arthritis. As a caution, strawberries are also one of the foods commonly associated with allergic reactions.

Icy Orange and Tomato Soup

Zesty refreshing flavor – a snap to make.

2 cups	EACH orange and tomato juice	500 mL
½ cup	white wine	125 mL
1	lemon, juice of	5 mL
1 tsp.	EACH sugar and salt	5 mL
¼-½ tsp.	cayenne pepper	1-2 mL
	chopped cilantro OR parsley for garnish	

In a large pitcher, combine all ingredients, except cilantro. Chill. Serve ice cold in bowls or wine glasses. Garnish with cilantro.

Serves 4-6

Chilled Summer Vegetable Garden Soup

A bit tangy, this soup has wonderful flavor. It's quick and easy to make, but allow time for the flavors to mingle. A great soup for warm weather parties.

4½ cups	tomato juice	1.125 L
2	medium carrots, sliced	2
2	stalks celery, sliced	2
1 cup	seeded, chopped cucumber	250 mL
4	green onions, chopped	4
2	lemon slices (¼"/6 mm thick)	2
1 tsp.	celery salt	5 mL
1 tsp.	Worcestershire sauce	5 mL
¼ tsp.	hot pepper sauce	1 mL
	green onion for garnish	

Place all ingredients in a food processor or blender and process or blend until smooth. Chill 4-6 hours for flavors to blend. Serve chilled, garnished with green onion fans or finely chopped green onion. To store, refrigerate in a tightly covered container for up to 3 days.

Serves 4-6

Chunky Gazpacho

One of the many treasures of Spain – their classic Gazpacho. Serve cold garnished with garlic croûtons.

4 cups	tomato juice	1 L
⅓ cup	red wine vinegar	75 mL
1	large red OR green pepper, finely chopped	1
1	large English cucumber, finely chopped	1
4	medium tomatoes, diced	4
1	small onion, finely chopped	1
2	garlic cloves, minced	2
2 tbsp.	chopped chives	30 mL
	salt and pepper to taste	
¼ tsp.	paprika	1 mL
	garlic croûtons	

In a large bowl, stir together tomato juice and vinegar. Add peppers, cucumber, tomatoes, onion, garlic, chives and paprika. Stir to combine. Chill for at least 3 hours. Serve cold, garnished with croûtons.

Serves 4-6

Variation: Less traditional, but delicious – add a generous splash of Worcestershire sauce and Tabasco. ¼-⅓ cup (60-75 mL) of fresh lemon juice is also a good addition. For a special party, a shot of vodka in each serving makes this a **Gazpacho Caesar**.

Cucumber skin is rich in fiber and contains beneficial minerals including silica, potassium and magnesium. Cucumber juice is often recommended as a source of silicon to improve the complexion and the health of the skin; as well, the high water content of cucumbers makes them naturally hydrating – a must for glowing skin.

Spiced Carrot and Pineapple Soup

A great chilled soup for those hot days. A refreshing soup to serve before a summer barbecue.

1 lb.	carrots, sliced	500 g
¾ cup	water	175 mL
2 x 8 oz.	cans unsweetened crushed pineapple with juice	2 x 250 mL
1 cup	unsweetened orange juice	250 mL
½ tsp.	ground coriander	2 mL
¼ tsp.	ground cardamom	1 mL
¼ tsp.	ground ginger	1 mL
	plain yogurt and mint sprigs for garnish	

Combine carrots and water in a medium saucepan. Bring to a boil; cover, reduce heat and simmer for 15 minutes, or until carrots are tender. Drain and discard cooking water. Place cooked carrots, pineapple with juice, orange juice, coriander, cardamom and ginger in a food processor or blender; process or blend until smooth. Chill for 4-6 hours before serving. Serve soup chilled, garnished with plain yogurt and fresh mint. To store, refrigerate in a tightly covered container for up to 3 days.

Serves 4-6

An excellent source of antioxidants, carrots are the richest vegetable source of beta carotene. They help protect against many types of cancer (colon, bladder, prostate, cervix, esophagus, lung and larynx), heart disease and promote good vision, particularly night vision. Studies suggest that 1 carrot per day could reduce lung cancer rates by up to half.

Summer Borscht With Cabbage

Wonderful color with a rich beef flavor, this soup is great served cold or hot.

6-8	fresh beets, peeled and shredded	6-8
5 cups	beef stock	1.25 L
2	finely chopped onions	2
1	garlic clove, minced	1
1 cup	finely chopped cabbage	250 mL
½ tsp.	salt	2 mL
⅛ tsp.	pepper	0.5 mL
1 tbsp.	Worcestershire sauce	15 mL
2 tbsp.	lemon juice	3 mL
3-4	drops hot pepper sauce	3-4
	light sour cream for garnish (optional)	
	chopped parsley OR chives for garnish	

Peel and shred beets; place in a large saucepan or Dutch oven. Add beef stock, onions, garlic and cabbage. Set over medium-high heat and bring to a boil. Reduce heat to low and simmer, covered, until vegetables are very tender, 1-1½ hours. Add salt, pepper, Worcestershire sauce, lemon juice and hot pepper sauce; stir to combine. Remove from heat and chill for 6-8 hours. Serve cold soup with a dollop of sour cream topped with chopped parsley or chives.

Serves 6

Note: This soup may be served either hot or cold. If serving hot, add leftover beef chunks for a whole meal soup. If serving cold, soup can be strained or served as is; both versions are full of flavor.

Herbed Buttermilk Broccoli Soup

Hot or cold, this soup has a wonderful flavor. This is a light version of an old favorite.

2 cups	chopped broccoli, stems and florets	500 mL
2 cups	chicken stock	500 mL
1 cup	low-fat buttermilk	250 mL
1 tsp.	Worcestershire sauce	5 mL
½ tsp.	dried basil	2 mL
½ tsp.	dried tarragon	2 mL
½ tsp.	dried dillweed	2 mL
¼ tsp.	salt	1 mL
⅛ tsp.	pepper	0.5 mL
	grated Cheddar cheese OR	
	chopped chives for garnish	

In a large saucepan, over medium heat, cook broccoli in chicken stock for 5-8 minutes, or until tender. Refrigerate broccoli and stock until chilled. In a food processor or blender, purée chilled broccoli mixture, buttermilk, Worcestershire sauce and seasonings until smooth. Taste to adjust seasonings. Reheat just to serving temperature or chill and serve as a cold soup. Garnish hot soup with Cheddar cheese; garnish cold soup with chives.

Serves 4-6

Lower in fat than regular milk, buttermilk is high in potassium, Vitamin B12, calcium and riboflavin, plus a good source of phosphorus. It is more quickly digested than milk. It has more lactic acid than skim milk. To replace sour cream or butter, try putting buttermilk on baked or mashed potatoes. It also makes an excellent salad dressing or soup base.

Cream of Asparagus Soup

The smooth creamy flavor is deceptive – this is a healthier soup.

1 tbsp.	olive oil	15 mL
1	large onion, chopped	1
½ cup	chopped celery	125 mL
4 cups	chicken stock	1 L
1½ lbs.	fresh asparagus, cut into 1" (2.5 cm) pieces	750 g
2 cups	diced peeled potatoes	500 mL
1	garlic clove, minced	1
⅛ tsp.	pepper	0.5 mL
½ cup	low-fat milk	125 mL
1 tbsp.	minced fresh parsley (optional)	15 mL

In a large saucepan or Dutch oven, over medium heat, heat oil and sauté onion and celery until tender. Add chicken stock, asparagus, potatoes, garlic and pepper. Bring to a boil. Reduce heat to low; cover and simmer for 20-25 minutes, or until vegetables are tender. Remove from heat and allow to cool. Pour cooled vegetable mixture into a food processor or blender; blend or process until smooth. Return soup to pan; add milk and cook over low heat until heated through. Serve immediately. Sprinkle with fresh parsley if desired.

Serves 6

Note: To help eliminate the fat content in creamy soups with minimum change in flavor or texture, a potato cooked with the rest of the ingredients will add flavor and help to thicken the soup. In this way you can eliminate the heavy cream or thickened, butter-based sauces.

For other soups, just cook a scrubbed, diced potato in enough water to cover. When fork tender, purée the potato in its cooking water and stir it into the soup. Cooked, puréed cauliflower is also a good thickening, flavoring option.

Cream of Carrot Soup

A lemon zest and parsley garnish make this delicious soup sparkle.

6	carrots, peeled and chopped	6
½ cup	chopped onion	125 mL
½ cup	chopped celery	125 mL
2	garlic cloves, minced	2
1	bay leaf	1
1 tbsp.	olive oil	15 mL
3 cups	chicken stock, divided	750 mL
1 tsp.	sugar	5 mL
½ tsp.	seasoning salt	2 mL
⅛ tsp.	pepper	0.5 mL
1 tbsp.	grated lemon zest	15 mL
1 tbsp.	chopped fresh parsley	15 mL

In a large saucepan, combine carrots, onion, celery, garlic, bay leaf and oil. Cover and cook over very low heat until carrots are tender, about 8-10 minutes. Cool slightly; remove bay leaf. Add 1 cup (250 mL) chicken stock to carrot mixture. In a blender or food processor, process for about 1 minute, or until smooth. Return to saucepan and add remaining chicken stock, sugar, seasoning salt and pepper. Place over medium heat and, stirring often, heat through. Pour into soup bowls; sprinkle each serving with lemon zest and parsley.

Serves 3-4

Variation: Nutmeg, cinnamon, cumin and curry powder all add another dimension to carrot soup. Let your tastebuds be your guide.

Soups & Salads

Chilled Creamy Melon and Mango Soup, page 26
Gorgonzola and Pear Salad, page 58
Herbed Buttermilk Biscuits, page 12

Cream of Potato Soup with Cheddar

This is a great favorite – comforting and flavorful.

2 cups	potatoes, peeled, diced	500 mL
1	chopped onion	1
½ cup	chopped celery	125 mL
3 cups	chicken stock	750 mL
⅛ tsp.	pepper	0.5 mL
3 tbsp.	cornstarch	45 mL
1½ cups	evaporated low-fat milk	375 mL
	salt to taste	
½ cup	shredded low-fat Cheddar cheese	125 mL

In a large saucepan, combine potatoes, onion, celery, chicken stock and pepper. Bring to a boil over medium-high heat. Reduce heat; cover and simmer for 15-20 minutes, or until vegetables are tender. Combine cornstarch and ¼ cup (60 mL) of the milk until smooth; stir into potato mixture. Add remaining milk and salt to taste. Bring to a boil; cook and stir for 2 minutes, or until thickened. Remove from heat; stir in cheese until melted. Serve immediately.

Serves 4-6

Potatoes, without added fat, are a very healthy food – low calorie, high fiber, and offering significant protection against cardiovascular disease and cancer. They are a very good source of Vitamin C, and a good source of Vitamin B₆, copper, potassium, manganese and fiber. They contain antioxidants and blood pressure-lowering compounds called kukoamines. Potato skins contain most of the fiber in potatoes – so eat the skins for the most cholesterol-lowering, positive elimination system effects.

Vegetable Corn Chowder

A delicious corn chowder filled with vegetables. It is a great main-meal soup.

2 cups	chicken stock	500 mL
2 cups	chopped broccoli	500 mL
1 tbsp.	olive oil	15 mL
1 cup	sliced fresh mushrooms	250 mL
½ cup	finely chopped onion	125 mL
½ cup	finely chopped celery	125 mL
2 tbsp.	all-purpose flour	30 mL
1½ cups	skim milk	375 mL
2 cups	whole kernel corn	500 mL
2 tbsp.	chopped pimiento	30 mL

In a large saucepan, over medium heat, cook chicken stock and broccoli for 5-8 minutes; set aside. In a frying pan over medium heat, heat oil and cook mushrooms, onion and celery for about 4 minutes, or until softened. Blend in flour; cook, stirring constantly, for 2 minutes. Slowly add milk; cook, stirring constantly, for 2 minutes, until smooth and thickened. Add broccoli mixture, corn and pimiento. Heat until corn and broccoli are cooked and tender. Serve immediately.

Serves 4-6

Variations: For a **Spicy Corn Chowder**, add ½ tsp. (2 mL) or more of Worcestershire sauce and up to ½ tsp. (2 mL) of hot pepper sauce.

Hearty Pasta and Bean Soup

A thick, very satisfying supper dish that is quick and easy to make.

1 tbsp.	olive oil	15 mL
½ cup	chopped celery	125 mL
½ cup	chopped onion	125 mL
2	garlic cloves, minced	2
28 oz.	can tomatoes with juice	796 mL
4 cups	chicken stock	1 L
1 cup	water	250 mL
½ tsp.	EACH dried basil and oregano	2 mL
¼ tsp.	pepper	1 mL
3 x 19 oz.	cans great northern OR pinto beans, drained and rinsed	3 x 540 mL
1 cup	uncooked macaroni	250 mL
1 tbsp.	minced fresh parsley	15 mL

In a large saucepan, heat oil and sauté celery, onion and garlic until tender. Add tomatoes with juice; simmer for 5 minutes. Add stock, water and seasonings. Bring to a boil; cook for 5 minutes. Add beans and macaroni; return to a boil. Reduce heat; simmer, uncovered, for 15 minutes, or until macaroni is tender. Sprinkle with parsley. Serve immediately.

Serves 6-8

Oregano contains numerous phytonutrients that function as potent antioxidants. The volatile oils, thymol and carvacrol, in oregano make it a very effective anti-bacterial. As well, oregano is a very good source of manganese, iron and dietary fiber. It is also a good source of omega-3 fatty acids, calcium, vitamins A and C.

Garlic and Onion Soup

Garlic and onions both contain powerful antioxidants and are full of flavor. This is a very comforting soup when you have a cold.

2 tbsp.	butter OR olive oil	30 mL
2 cups	chopped onions	500 mL
30	peeled garlic cloves	30
2 tbsp.	all-purpose flour	30 mL
5 cups	chicken stock	1.25 L
1 cup	yogurt OR light cream	250 mL
½ cup	dry sherry	125 mL
1 tsp.	dried thyme	4 mL
1	small bay leaf	
3 slices	whole-grain bread, torn into pieces	
	salt and pepper to taste	

Melt butter in a large pot over medium heat. Add onions and garlic. Cover; cook until onions are tender but not brown, stirring occasionally, about 10 minutes. Stir in flour; stir 2 minutes. Add stock, yogurt, sherry, thyme and bay leaf. Bring just to a boil. Reduce heat to medium-low; simmer, uncovered, until garlic is very tender, about 15 minutes. Discard bay leaf. Working in batches, purée soup with bread in a food processor until smooth. Return to pot. Season with salt and pepper; heat and serve.

Serves 6

Variations:

Use ready-peeled garlic if the thought of peeling 30 cloves is overwhelming.

OR use chopped garlic instead of whole cloves and leave the soup chunky rather than puréeing it. Place bread or croûtons on individual servings; add grated Swiss cheese and broil until cheese is bubbly.

OR, for an Asian flavor, omit the sherry and cream. Add ½ tsp. hot pepper flakes, plus a garnish of cilantro and a squeeze of lime for each serving. You can also add a 28 oz. (796 mL) can of diced tomatoes.

Campbell's Lodge Tangy Asparagus and Crab Soup

We were served this soup while visiting relatives at their lodge. The ginger and red pepper combination gives it an amazing flavor.

4 cups	chicken stock	1 L
¼ tsp.	ground ginger	1 mL
2 cups	asparagus pieces, cut diagonally into ½" (1.3 cm) pieces	500 mL
¼ cup	chopped onions	60 mL
½ cup	chopped celery	125 mL
3 tbsp.	white wine vinegar	45 mL
¼ tsp.	crushed red pepper	1 mL
8-12 oz.	cooked crab meat OR imitation crab, cut diagonally	250-340 g

In a large saucepan over medium heat, bring chicken stock and ginger to a boil. Add asparagus, onion, celery, vinegar and crushed pepper; simmer for 5 minutes, or until asparagus is tender-crisp. Add crab meat and simmer for 5 minutes, or until seafood is hot. Serve immediately.

Serves 4-6

Asparagus is low in calories and a good source of folic acid, vitamins A and C, and the B vitamins, plus potassium. One serving per day of asparagus (1 cup/250 mL) supplies about 60 percent of the daily recommended amount of folate, which is essential to cardiovascular health. Asparagus also has a diuretic effect and helps to promote a healthy urinary and intestinal tract.

Salmon and Shrimp Soup with Rice

Like a jambalaya, this succulent soup is served with rice.

1 tbsp.	olive oil	15 mL
½ cup	chopped onion	125 mL
½ cup	chopped red OR green pepper	125 mL
½ cup	chopped celery	125 mL
½ cup	sliced mushrooms	125 mL
1	garlic clove, minced	1
28 oz.	can tomatoes with juice	796 mL
2 cups	chicken stock	500 mL
½ tsp.	pepper	2 mL
½ tsp.	dried thyme	2 mL
½ tsp.	dried basil	2 mL
1½ cups	fresh peas, or frozen	375 mL
¾ lb.	salmon, cut into 1" (2.5 cm) pieces	350 g
½ lb.	shrimp, peeled, deveined	250 g
3 cups	hot cooked rice	750 mL

In a large saucepan or Dutch oven, heat oil over medium-high heat; cook onion, peppers, celery, mushrooms and garlic until tender-crisp. Stir in tomatoes with juice, chicken stock, pepper, thyme and basil; bring to a boil. Reduce heat; simmer, uncovered, for 10 minutes. Stir in peas, salmon and shrimp; simmer for 10-15 minutes, or until fish flakes with a fork. Serve in large soup bowls with rice on top of the soup. Allow ½ cup (125 mL) of cooked rice per serving.

Serves 6

Rice is low in calories and contains no cholesterol. It is the basic food staple for 6 out of 10 people in the world. Rice has an almost indefinite shelf life.

Mom's Chicken Noodle Soup

A "from scratch" recipe – cooking the chicken in the chicken stock gives this soup wonderful flavor. It is one of our family favorites. An absolute must when you are not feeling "up to par."

8 cups	chicken stock	2 L
½ lb.	boneless chicken, cut into bite-sized pieces	250 g
1½ cups	uncooked medium egg noodles	375 mL
1 cup	sliced carrots	250 mL
¾ cup	chopped onion	175 mL
¾ cup	sliced celery	175 mL
1 tsp.	dried dillweed	5 mL
¼ tsp.	pepper	1 mL

In a large saucepan, combine chicken stock, chicken, noodles, carrots, onion, celery, dillweed and pepper. Set over medium-high heat and bring to a boil. Reduce heat; simmer for 30-45 minutes, or until chicken and noodles are cooked. Serve immediately.

Serves 8

Grandma's chicken soup is famed in folklore for its healing powers. Scientists are proving grandma right. An amino acid released from chicken during cooking helps to treat some respiratory illnesses by providing healthy nutrients, hydration and easily absorbed calories. Chicken is a good source of niacin (vitamin B$_3$), which protects cells against DNA damage, and selenium, which aids the immune system. Scientists at UCLA Medical School recommend adding garlic, thyme and ginger to act as mild anti-bacterials, helping to prevent secondary infections and reducing congestion, making breathing easier.

Tomato Chicken Vegetable Soup

A quick and easy soup using cooked chicken, this robust mix of vegetables and chicken makes a satisfying supper dish.

4 cups	chicken stock	1 L
2 cups	frozen corn	500 mL
2	stalks celery, chopped	2
2	carrots, diced	2
1	onion, chopped	1
2 cups	cubed cooked chicken	500 mL
19 oz.	can tomatoes with juice	540 mL
1 tsp.	dried parsley	5 mL
¼ tsp.	salt	1 mL
⅛ tsp.	pepper	0.5 mL

In a large saucepan, combine chicken stock, corn, celery, carrots and onion; place over medium-high heat and bring to a boil. Reduce heat to low; cover and simmer for 25-30 minutes, or until vegetables are tender. Stir in chicken, tomatoes, parsley, salt and pepper; heat through. Serve immediately.

Serves 4

Variation: For a **Hearty Spinach Chicken Soup**, omit the corn and celery and add 3-4 minced garlic cloves, 1-2 tbsp. (15-30 mL) minced fresh ginger and 1 large sweet potato, peeled and chopped, to the stock and vegetables. Add 6 cups (1.5 L) packed, torn spinach and 1-2 tsp. (5-10 mL) hot pepper sauce with the chicken and tomatoes. Cook until spinach is wilted.

Celery was once used exclusively as a medicinal herb. In Chinese medicine, it has long been used to reduce blood pressure. It also helps to lower cholesterol and has a diuretic effect, which helps the body get rid of excess fluid. Celery is an excellent source of vitamin C, which helps support the immune system, reducing the risk of heart disease, stroke and cancer.

Chicken, Vegetables and Rice Soup with Lime

A hearty "from scratch" soup that is a main-dish meal. The fresh parsley gives this soup great flavor.

8 cups	chicken stock	2 L
1	medium onion, chopped	1
1 cup	sliced celery	250 mL
1 cup	sliced carrots	250 mL
¼ cup	snipped fresh parsley	60 mL
¼ tsp.	pepper	1 mL
½ tsp.	dried thyme	2 mL
1	bay leaf	1
1½ cups	boneless chicken, cut into bite-sized pieces	375 mL
2 cups	cooked rice	500 mL
2 tbsp.	fresh lime juice	30 mL

In a large saucepan or Dutch oven, combine stock, onion, celery, carrots, parsley, pepper, thyme and bay leaf; set over medium-high heat and bring to a boil. Reduce heat; simmer, uncovered, for 10 minutes. Add chicken; simmer, uncovered, for 25-35 minutes, or until chicken is cooked. Remove soup from heat and discard bay leaf. Stir in rice and lime juice; place over medium heat and reheat to serving temperature. Serve immediately.

Serves 8-10

Thyme has a history in natural medicine in connection with chest and respiratory problems. The volatile oil in thyme, as well as the variety of flavenoids it contains, makes it an important antioxidant food. Thyme is an excellent source of iron and manganese; a very good source of calcium; and a good source of dietary fiber.

Ham, Cabbage and Potato Soup

Meat, potatoes, and vegetables in one tasty soup. A great use for leftover ham.

1 tbsp.	olive oil	15 mL
1	small onion, chopped	1
½ cup	chopped celery	125 mL
5 cups	chicken stock	1.25 L
3 cups	chopped cabbage	750 mL
2 cups	diced potatoes	500 mL
2	garlic cloves, minced	2
⅛ tsp.	pepper	0.5 mL
2 cups	cubed fully cooked ham	500 mL

In a large saucepan or Dutch oven, over medium heat, heat oil and sauté onion and celery until tender. Add chicken stock, cabbage, potatoes, garlic and pepper. Cover and bring to a boil; reduce heat to low and simmer for 25-30 minutes, or until potatoes are tender. Stir in ham; heat through. Serve immediately.

Serves 6-8

Cabbage contains beneficial phytochemicals which help protect against breast, lung, stomach and colon cancers. It is also an excellent source of vitamin C. Raw cabbage juice has been shown to be effective in treating peptic ulcers. Related to broccoli, kale and brussels sprouts, cabbage has long been used as a food and a medicine.

Tomato Beef Soup

A quick and easy-to-prepare, robust mix of ground beef, vegetables and pasta –
a main-dish soup.

1½ lbs.	extra-lean ground beef	375 mL
1 cup	chopped onion	250 mL
½ cup	chopped celery	125 mL
2	garlic cloves, minced	2
28 oz.	can tomatoes with juice	796 mL
6 cups	beef stock	1.5 L
¼ tsp.	pepper	1 mL
½ cup	uncooked orzo OR any small pasta	125 mL
1½ cups	frozen mixed vegetables	375 mL

In a large saucepan over medium-high heat, cook ground beef, onion, celery and garlic until beef is brown and no pink is showing, stirring to separate meat. Drain off all fat and set beef mixture aside. Purée tomatoes with juice in a blender or food processor. Add tomatoes, beef stock and pepper to meat mixture. Place over medium-high heat and bring to a boil; reduce heat to low and simmer, uncovered, for 20 minutes. Add pasta and vegetables and simmer for an additional 15-25 minutes. Serve immediately.

Serves 6-8

Main-Dish Beef Barley Soup

A thick tomato-based hearty soup, just add a whole-wheat roll and dinner is complete.

1½ cups	tomato juice OR vegetable juice cocktail	375 mL
1 cup	water	250 mL
2 cups	beef stock	500 mL
¾ cup	tomato sauce	175 mL
½-¾ cup	pearl barley	125-175 mL
2	large carrots, diced	2
2	large potatoes, diced	2
1 tsp.	Worcestershire sauce	5 mL
½ tsp.	salt	2 mL
¼ tsp.	pepper	1 mL
1½ cups	cubed, cooked lean beef	375 mL

In a large saucepan or stockpot, combine tomato juice, water, beef stock, tomato sauce, barley, carrot, potato, Worcestershire sauce and seasonings. Bring to a boil over high heat. Reduce heat to low and simmer, covered, for 1 hour. Add beef and cook for an additional 30 minutes.

Serves 4

Beef Stock

Roasting the bones before simmering gives a dark, richly colored stock.

3 lbs.	meaty beef bones	1.5 kg
10 cups	water	2.5 L
4	sprigs parsley	4
2	onions, coarsely chopped	2
4	stalks celery, chopped into chunks	4
3	garlic cloves, coarsely chopped	3
3	carrots, chopped into chunks	3
1	bay leaf	1
½ tsp.	dried thyme	2 mL
¼ tsp.	pepper	1 mL
½ tsp.	salt	2 mL

Preheat oven to 425°F (220°C). Place bones in a large shallow roasting pan; roast in oven for about 1 hour, or until well browned, turning occasionally. Transfer meat and bones to a large stockpot or Dutch oven. Add water, parsley, onion, celery, garlic, carrot and seasonings. Bring to a boil; skim off foam and discard. Reduce heat to low; cook, covered, for 3 hours, or until meat is very tender. Lift out meat; reserve for another use. Remove bones and discard. Strain liquid through a sieve; press down on vegetables to extract as much flavor as possible. Chill stock; remove fat from surface. Stock can be refrigerated for 2-3 days, or frozen for up to 3 months.

Makes 7-8 cups (1.75-2 L)

Stock is the base for soups and sauces, as well as a moistener for many dishes. Freeze stock in usable quantities, e.g., 2 tbsp. (30 mL) amounts, freeze in ice cube trays; 1 cup (250 mL) amounts, freeze in yogurt cups or paper cups. Then remove the frozen stock from the containers, pack in plastic bags and store in the freezer.

Chicken Stock

The best soups are made with the best stocks – a classic!

3 lbs.	chicken	1.5 kg
10 cups	water	2.5 L
4	sprigs parsley	4
1	onion, coarsely chopped	1
2	carrot, chopped into chunks	2
4	stalk celery, chopped into chunks	4
1	bay leaf	1
½ tsp.	pepper	2 mL
¼ tsp.	dried marjoram	1 mL
½ tsp.	salt	2 mL

In a large stockpot or Dutch oven, place chicken, water, parsley, onion, carrot, celery and seasonings. Bring to a boil; skim off foam and discard. Cook, covered, on low heat for 2-3 hours, or until chicken is tender. Remove chicken; reserve. Strain liquid through sieve; press down on vegetables to extract as much flavor as possible. Chill stock; remove fat from surface. Stock can be refrigerated for 2-3 days or frozen for up to 3 months. Reserved chicken can be used in various recipes, depending on the type of meat used.

Makes 8-10 cups (2-2.5 L)

Chicken pieces to use: backs, necks, and wings – this is economical and the small pieces of meat will provide flavor. The meat can be added to soups after it is strained from the stock.

Legs, thighs, breasts – cook these pieces just until tender, then you will have cooked chicken for another use.

Stewing hen – provides wonderful flavor for stock base, as well as left-over chicken for other uses. However, due to the old age of the hen, this type requires the longest cooking time.

Note: Bones are the most important ingredient in any stock. They contribute flavor and substance. In recipes calling for chicken broth or stock, commercial products can also be substituted, but they generally are higher in sodium. With homemade stock, soup has more appetite appeal.

Salads

Aspic
Fruit & Greens
Vegetables & Beans
Main-Course
Dressings

Spicy Tomato Aspic

As attractive as it is delicious, this salad teams up as well with quiche as it does with roast beef. It has a wonderful spicy, tomato flavor.

2 tbsp.	unflavored gelatin (2 x 7 g env.)	30 mL
3 cups	vegetable juice cocktail, divided	750 mL
1 tbsp.	grated onion	15 mL
1	garlic clove, minced	1
¼ tsp.	hot pepper sauce	1 mL
2 tsp.	Worcestershire sauce	10 mL
¼ tsp.	salt	1 mL
¾ cup	chopped red OR green pepper	175 mL
¾ cup	chopped celery	175 mL
2-3	lettuce leaves	2-3

In a medium saucepan, sprinkle gelatin over 1 cup (250 mL) of juice; let stand 1 minute. Set saucepan over low heat and cook, stirring constantly until gelatin dissolves. Stir in onion, garlic, hot pepper sauce, Worcestershire sauce, salt and remaining 2 cups (500 mL) of juice. Chill in refrigerator until mixture is the consistency of unbeaten egg whites. Fold in peppers and celery; pour into an oiled 4-cup (1 L) ring mold. Cover and refrigerate for 6-8 hours. To serve, unmold onto a lettuce-lined serving plate.

Serves 4-6

Colorful bell peppers are rich sources of vitamins C and A, powerful antioxidants. They contain folic acid and vitamin B₆ which can also reduce the risk of heart disease, stroke and several cancers. Red peppers contain lycopene which is important in reducing cancers of the prostate, cervix, bladder and pancreas. They also contain phytonutrients which have been shown to protect against macular degeneration.

Citrus Sprout Salad with Toasted Almonds

A light and refreshing salad, this is a nice first course for a dinner party or team it up with a platter of cold meats and nippy cheeses for a casual crowd.

4 cups	torn lettuce	1 L
1 cup	bean sprouts, washed, patted dry	250 mL
1	pink grapefruit, peeled, sectioned	1
2	oranges, peeled, sectioned	2
½ cup	sliced celery	125 mL
¼ cup	toasted, slivered almonds	60 mL

Tangy Orange Dressing:

3 tbsp.	unsweetened orange juice	45 mL
1 tbsp.	cider vinegar	15 mL
1 tbsp.	olive oil	15 mL
½ tsp.	celery salt	2 mL
1 tbsp.	sugar	15 mL
4-5	drops hot pepper sauce	4-5

In a large salad bowl, combine lettuce, bean sprouts, grapefruit, oranges, celery and almonds.

Dressing: In a shaker or small jar with a tight-fitting lid, combine all dressing ingredients. Cover and shake until well mixed. Pour over salad and toss well.

Serves 4

Pictured on the front cover.

Sprout and Mushroom Salad with Chow Mein Noodles

A light, crisp salad that is great served with pork or chicken.

8-10 cups	torn Romaine lettuce	2-2.5 L
4 cups	fresh bean sprouts	1 L
3 cups	sliced mushrooms	750 mL
½ cup	chopped green onion	125 mL
½ cup	sliced celery	125 mL
1	chopped red pepper	1
½ cup	sliced radishes	125 mL

Oil and Vinegar Dressing:

2 tbsp.	soy sauce	30 mL
2 tbsp.	rice vinegar	30 mL
4 tsp.	olive oil	20 mL
⅛ tsp.	pepper	0.5 mL
¼ tsp.	salt	1 mL
1 cup	chow mein noodles	250 mL

In a large bowl, combine lettuce, bean sprouts, mushrooms, onion, celery, peppers and radishes; toss to combine.

Dressing: In a small bowl or shaker, combine soy sauce, vinegar, oil, pepper and salt; whisk or shake well to combine and pour over salad.

Toss salad with dressing and sprinkle chow mein noodles over top. Serve immediately.

Serves 8-10

Spinach and Mushroom Salad with Hot Onion Dressing

This is a different but delicious salad. If you are a spinach lover, you will love this one!

¼ lb.	sliced bacon	125 g

Hot Onion Dressing:

2 tbsp.	bacon drippings	30 mL
½ cup	chopped onions	125 mL
2 tbsp.	all-purpose flour	30 mL
1 cup	beef stock OR chicken stock	250 mL
⅓ cup	red wine vinegar	75 mL
8 cups	torn spinach leaves	2 L
2 cups	sliced mushrooms	500 mL

In a large frying pan over medium-high heat, cook bacon until crisp; drain reserving 2 tbsp. (30 mL) drippings. Crumble bacon; set aside.

Dressing: In reserved drippings, over medium heat, cook onions until tender. Stir in flour; cook for 1 minute. Stir in stock and vinegar; heat to boiling. Reduce heat; cook until slightly thickened.

In a large bowl, combine torn spinach leaves and mushrooms. Pour hot dressing over salad, tossing to coat well. Sprinkle with crumbled bacon. Serve immediately.

Serves 6-8

Spinach has been identified as having 13 different flavonoid compounds that work as antioxidants and as anti-cancer agents. The vitamin K in spinach is important in helping to prevent osteoporosis and vitamins C and A provide cardiovascular protection as well as protection from colon cancer and inflammatory conditions such as asthma and arthritis. Better eyesight, more energy and improved brain function are more benefits of spinach consumption.

Tossed Vegetable Salad with Garbanzo Beans

A great tossed vegetable salad with a Mediterranean flair, this is a favorite in our family. Just add a whole-wheat roll and it makes a great luncheon dish.

1	head torn iceberg lettuce	1
19 oz.	can garbanzo beans, drained and rinsed	540 mL
1 cup	diced tomatoes	250 mL
1 cup	sliced celery	250 mL
1 cup	sliced radishes	250 mL
1 cup	sliced kalamata olives	250 mL
½ cup	low-fat Cheddar cheese	125 mL

In a large salad bowl, combine all ingredients; toss well. Serve with your favorite salad dressing, or try Italian Herb Dressing or Dill and Onion Vinaigrette on page 80.

Serves 4-6

Variation: Substitute crumbled feta cheese for the Cheddar.

Garbanzo beans (chickpeas) are a good source of fiber, which lowers cholesterol and prevents the rapid rise of blood sugar levels. They combine with whole-grains (e.g. rice) to provide a high-quality, fat-free protein. They are also an excellent source of molybdenum, a trace mineral which detoxifies sulites (preservatives) which may cause headaches, disorientation and rapid heartbeat.

Toasted Pistachio and Romaine Salad with Cranberry Vinaigrette

Fabulous flavors and great color – this salad is sure to impress.

Cranberry Vinaigrette:

¼ cup	cranberry cocktail	60 mL
1 tbsp.	white wine vinegar	15 mL
¼ cup	chopped green onion	60 mL
1 tsp.	EACH Dijon mustard and maple syrup	5 mL
⅛ tsp.	EACH salt and pepper	0.5 mL
2 tbsp.	olive oil	30 mL
½ cup	shelled pistachio nuts	125 mL
6	strips bacon, cooked crisp, crumbled	6
8 cups	torn romaine lettuce	2 L
1 cup	sliced mushrooms	250 mL
½ cup	dried cranberries	125 mL

Cranberry Vinaigrette: In a small bowl, whisk together cranberry cocktail, vinegar, green onion, mustard, maple syrup, salt and pepper. Slowly whisk in oil. Set aside.

Preheat oven to 350°F (180°C). Spread shelled pistachios on a baking sheet; toast in oven for 5-8 minutes, or until fragrant. Remove from oven and set aside to cool; chop coarsely.

In a frying pan over medium-high heat, cook bacon until browned and crisp, about 4-7 minutes. Transfer to paper towel to drain and cool; crumble and set aside.

Add torn romaine lettuce to a large salad bowl; toss with cranberry vinaigrette. Add pistachios, mushrooms, and cranberries; toss again. Sprinkle crumbled bacon over and serve immediately.

Serves 6-8

Pictured on page 103.

Gorgonzola and Pear Salad

If you like blue cheese, this salad is superbly satisfying as a lunchtime salad or teamed with a barbecued steak for a full-dinner menu.

Creamy Lemon Dressing:

⅓ cup	low-fat mayonnaise	75 mL
1 tbsp.	liquid honey	15 mL
3 tbsp.	fresh lemon juice, divided	45 mL
1 tsp.	grated lemon zest	5 mL
1 tbsp.	milk	15 mL
¼ tsp.	salt	1 mL
8 cups	lettuce	2 L
1	apple, cored, thinly sliced	1
3	pears, cored, thinly sliced	3
½ cup	thinly sliced celery	125 mL
¼ cup	toasted, coarsely chopped walnuts	60 mL
½ cup	crumbled Gorgonzola OR mild blue cheese	125 mL

Dressing: In a small bowl, blend mayonnaise, honey, 1 tbsp. (15 mL) lemon juice, lemon zest, milk and salt until smooth; set aside.

Wash and dry lettuce. Wash and core apple and pears; slice thinly and toss with remaining lemon juice in a large serving bowl. Tear lettuce into bowl; add celery and toss until mixed. Sprinkle walnuts and crumbled cheese over salad and drizzle with dressing.

Serves 4

Pictured on page 35.

Tomatoes and Green Onions in Herbed Vinaigrette

This delicious salad takes only minutes to prepare. Allow tomatoes to marinate for at least 2 hours to get the full flavor of the herbs.

6	large tomatoes, cut into wedges	6
½ cup	thinly sliced green onions	125 mL

Herbed Vinaigrette:

⅓ cup	olive oil	75 mL
¼ cup	red wine vinegar OR cider vinegar	60 mL
¼ cup	minced fresh parsley	60 mL
3	garlic cloves, minced	3
½ tsp.	salt	2 mL
1 tbsp.	snipped fresh thyme or 1 tsp. (5 mL) dried	15 mL
¼ tsp.	pepper	1 mL

Place tomatoes and onions in a shallow serving bowl.

Vinaigrette: In a small bowl, combine oil, vinegar, parsley, garlic, salt, thyme and pepper; mix well. Pour vinaigrette over tomatoes.

Cover and refrigerate for at least 2 hours or overnight.

Serves 8-10

Parsley contains volatile oils and flavenoids which help in cancer prevention and function as potent antioxidants. It is also an excellent source of vitamin C, beta-carotene and folic acid, which protect against heart attack, stroke and colon and cervix cancers. Parsley is also a renowned breath freshener and palate cleanser.

Layered Greek Salad With Tzatziki Dressing

This salad is very colorful and showy when presented in a glass salad bowl. If you like Greek salad, you will love this one!!

3 cups	torn spinach	750 mL
3 cups	torn romaine lettuce	750 mL
½ cup	sliced pitted kalamata olives	125 mL
1 cup	alfalfa sprouts	250 mL
1 cup	chopped tomatoes	250 mL
1 cup	chopped green OR red peppers	250 mL
1 cup	crumbled feta cheese	250 mL

Tzatziki Dressing:

1 cup	low-fat plain yogurt	250 mL
1	cucumber, shredded	1
3	garlic cloves, minced	3
½ tsp.	dried oregano	2 mL

Combine torn spinach and lettuce. In the bottom of a large glass salad bowl, place half of the spinach and lettuce mixture. Layer the remaining salad ingredients in the following order: olives, alfalfa sprouts, tomatoes, peppers, feta cheese and remaining half of spinach and lettuce mixture.

In a small bowl, stir together yogurt, cucumber, garlic and oregano; mix well to combine. Spread dressing evenly over the salad, sealing dressing to the edge of the bowl. Cover tightly with plastic wrap. Chill up to 24 hours. Garnish with cucumber slices, tomatoes or sliced olives.

Serves 8

Red Cabbage Slaw with Tangy Blue Cheese Dressing

This salad can be made a day in advance and refrigerated. It can be turned into a nice luncheon dish by adding some cooked chicken breast, tuna or salmon.

Tangy Blue Cheese Dressing:

⅔ cup	light sour cream	150 mL
⅔ cup	low-fat plain yogurt	150 mL
¼ cup	cider vinegar	60 mL
1 tbsp.	low-fat mayonnaise	15 mL
4 tsp.	sugar	20 mL
1 tsp.	hot pepper sauce	5 mL
1 tsp.	salt	5 mL
⅓ cup	crumbled blue cheese	75 mL
8 cups	finely shredded red cabbage	2 L
½ cup	diced celery	125 mL
4	apples, thinly sliced	4
2	green OR red peppers, thinly sliced	2
¼ cup	toasted, chopped walnuts	60 mL

Dressing: In a large bowl, whisk together sour cream, yogurt, vinegar, mayonnaise, sugar, hot pepper sauce and salt; stir in blue cheese.

Add cabbage, celery, apples, peppers and walnuts to bowl and toss to combine well. Serve at room temperature or chilled.

Serves 8-10

Walnuts are one of the best sources of alpha-linolenic acid (omega-3 fatty acids). They are also a very good source of antioxidants, vitamins and fiber. A handful of walnuts daily can reduce heart disease risk by lowering LDL (bad) cholesterol, reducing inflammation and staving off hardening of the arteries. They can also help reduce insulin resistance and improve brain function.

Fruit and Cabbage Slaw

This unique combination of fruit and vegetables will complement any entrée from pasta to barbecued steak. Super for potluck suppers.

5 cups	shredded cabbage	1.25 L
10 oz.	can mandarin oranges, drained	284 mL
1 cup	sliced cauliflower	250 mL
8 oz.	can unsweetened pineapple slices, drained, chopped	227 g
½ cup	chopped celery	125 mL
½ cup	chopped cucumber	125 mL
¼ cup	sliced green onions	60 mL
½ cup	chopped green OR red pepper	125 mL

Mustard & Celery Seed Dressing:

⅔ cup	sugar	150 mL
⅓ cup	white vinegar	75 mL
⅓ cup	olive oil	75 mL
1 tbsp.	water	15 mL
1 tsp.	salt	5 mL
1 tsp.	prepared mustard	5 mL
½ tsp.	celery seed	2 mL

In a large bowl, toss together cabbage, oranges, cauliflower, pineapple, celery, cucumber, green onions and peppers.

Dressing: In a small bowl, combine all dressing ingredients; mix well.

Stir dressing into cabbage mixture. Cover and refrigerate for 2 hours. Toss again just before serving.

Serves 6-8

Make-Ahead Cabbage and Pineapple Slaw

A wonderful make-ahead favorite when you have a large gathering. Great for potluck suppers and block parties.

2 cups	shredded cabbage	500 mL
¼ cup	chopped green onion	60 mL
8 oz.	can sliced pineapple, drained, diced	250 g
½ cup	chopped green OR red pepper	125 mL
¼ cup	sliced stuffed olives	60 mL
½ cup	chopped celery	125 mL
½ tsp.	salt	2 mL
⅛ tsp.	pepper	0.5 mL

Creamy Yogurt Dressing:

⅓ cup	low-fat plain yogurt	75 mL
¼ cup	low-fat mayonnaise	60 mL
2 tbsp.	lemon juice	30 mL
4-5 drops	hot pepper sauce	4-5 drops

In a large salad bowl, combine cabbage, green onions, pineapple, peppers, stuffed olives and celery. Sprinkle with seasonings; toss lightly.

Dressing: In a small bowl, combine all dressing ingredients.

Pour dressing over cabbage mixture. Toss to combine; cover and refrigerate for 4-6 hours, or can be made the day before and refrigerated.

Serves 4-6

Variation: For **Yogurt Horseradish Dressing**, replace the lemon juice with 1 tbsp. (15 mL) cider vinegar and the hot pepper sauce with ¼ tsp. (1 mL) freshly ground black pepper. Add 1-2 tbsp. (15-30 mL) prepared horseradish. Mix as above.

Cauliflower, Pea and Water Chestnut Salad with Creamy Dill Dressing

An ideal make-ahead salad. The crunchy cauliflower and water chestnuts team up nicely with the green peas and red onions for a showy and delicious salad.

Creamy Dill Dressing:

½ cup	low-fat mayonnaise	125 mL
2 tbsp.	lemon juice	30 mL
½ tsp.	dried dillweed	2 mL
1½ cups	frozen peas, thawed	375 mL
3 cups	cauliflower florets	750 mL
8 oz.	can sliced water chestnuts, drained	227 mL
¼ cup	chopped red onion	60 mL
¼ cup	whole cashews	60 mL

Dressing: In a large salad bowl, combine mayonnaise, lemon juice and dillweed until well blended.

Add peas, cauliflower, water chestnuts and onion to dressing in salad bowl; mix well. Refrigerate for 2-4 hours. Just before serving sprinkle with cashews.

Serves 6-8

 Cauliflower, like other cruciferous vegetables (broccoli, cabbage, kale, etc.) has compounds which may help prevent cancer. These compounds also help the liver neutralize potentially toxic substances. The high levels of vitamin C in cauliflower helps protect against rheumatoid arthritis and acts as an anti-inflammatory.

Mixed Vegetables in Red Wine Vinaigrette

A very attractive make-ahead dish that is a vegetable and salad all in one. Use your favorite combination of vegetables.

2 cups	cauliflower florets	500 mL
2 cups	broccoli florets	500 mL
1 cup	small mushrooms	250 mL
½	red pepper, cut into strips	½
½	green pepper, cut into strips	½
½ cup	celery, diagonally sliced	125 mL
2	carrots, sliced	2
1	small red onion, sliced	1

Red Wine Vinaigrette:

1 cup	red wine vinegar	250 mL
1 tsp.	dried oregano	5 mL
1 tsp.	dried tarragon	5 mL
½ tsp.	EACH sugar and salt	2 mL
¼ tsp.	pepper	1 mL
¼ cup	olive oil	60mL

In a large bowl, combine all vegetables.

Vinaigrette: In a small saucepan heat vinegar and seasonings to boiling point; remove from heat and add oil.

Pour vinaigrette over vegetables. Refrigerate for 24 hours before serving. Stir vegetables 4-5 times through this period.

Serves 8-10

Italian-Style Vegetable Salad

This salad has great crunch. Food with an Italian flair tops our list of favorites. Enjoy this salad with spaghetti and meatballs.

2 cups	broccoli florets	500 mL
1½ cups	sliced mushrooms	375 mL
1 cup	cherry tomatoes, halved	250 mL
1 cup	sliced celery	250 mL
1	small red onion, coarsely chopped	1
1	small red OR green pepper, thinly sliced	1
½-¾ cup	sliced kalamata olives	125-175 mL
½ cup	sliced water chestnuts	125 mL
⅓ cup	calorie-reduced Italian salad dressing (see page 80 or use a commercial dressing)	75 mL
¼ tsp.	pepper	1 mL

In a large salad bowl, combine all ingredients. Toss gently to coat. Cover and refrigerate for 6-8 hours, or overnight. To serve, spoon salad into serving bowl using a slotted spoon.

Serves 6

White button mushrooms contain the antioxidant ergothioneine which protects against chronic disease and has been shown to have anticancer properties. Mushrooms are an excellent source of selenium, riboflavin, pantothenic acid, copper, niacin, potassium and phosphorus. They are also a good source of manganese, iron, a variety of B complex vitamins and zinc. Of the thousands of mushroom species, shiitake, maitake and reishi have been called medicinal mushrooms. They all boost immune function and support cardiovascular health.

Garden Vegetable Toss with Parmesan

Garlic lemony dressing brings out the best in all of the vegetables in this salad.

1 cup	thinly sliced carrots	250 mL
1 cup	thinly sliced kohlrabi	250 mL
1 cup	snow peas	250 mL
1 cup	thinly sliced zucchini	250 mL
½ cup	sliced green onions	125 mL
½ cup	sliced celery	125 mL
½ cup	chopped red pepper	125 mL
½ cup	chopped green pepper	125 mL
1 cup	sliced kalamata olives	250 mL

Lemon Cider Dressing:

6 tbsp.	olive oil	90 mL
4 tsp.	lemon juice	20 mL
1 tbsp.	cider vinegar	15 mL
1 tbsp.	minced fresh parsley	15 mL
1 tsp.	sugar	5 mL
2	garlic cloves, minced	2
⅛ tsp.	EACH salt and pepper	0.5 mL
½ cup	shredded Parmesan cheese	125 mL

In a large salad bowl, combine carrots, kohlrabi, snow peas, zucchini, onions, celery, red and green peppers and olives.

Dressing: In a shaker or a jar with a tight-fitting lid, combine oil, lemon juice, vinegar, parsley, sugar, garlic, salt and pepper; shake well.

Pour dressing over vegetable mixture and toss to coat. Refrigerate for 1 hour. Just before serving, sprinkle with Parmesan cheese.

Serves 8-10

Layered Vegetable Salad

This colorful, crunchy salad is a perfect make-ahead dish when expecting a crowd. A vegetable and salad in one, it presents beautifully in a large glass salad bowl.

4	slices bacon, cooked crisp, crumbled	4
1½ cups	potatoes, boiled, cooled, cut into ½" (1.3 cm) cubes	375 mL
2 cups	corn kernels, boiled and cooled	500 mL
2 cups	shredded red cabbage	500 mL
1 cup	frozen green peas	250 mL
2 cups	cherry tomatoes, halved	500 mL
1 cup	sliced baby carrots	250 mL
2 cups	snow peas	500 mL
1	large green OR red pepper, cut into thin strips	1
2 cups	low-fat mayonnaise	500 mL
1 cup	light sour cream	250 mL
½ cup	chopped green onions	125 mL

Cook bacon in frying pan or microwave until crisp. Drain on paper towels, then crumble and refrigerate. Boil potatoes in water until tender; drain, cool, and cut into ½" (1.3 cm) cubes. Boil corn in water 3 minutes, drain and allow to cool.

In a large 6-quart (6 L) glass bowl, layer vegetables as follows: cabbage, frozen green peas, tomatoes, potatoes, carrots, snow peas, corn and peppers. In a small bowl, combine mayonnaise, sour cream and green onions to make dressing. Spread dressing over salad; cover with plastic wrap and refrigerate for 6 hours or overnight. Before serving, garnish with crumbled bacon.

Serves 12

Main Course Salad

Peach and Chicken Salad with Orange Yogurt Dressing, page 77
Tangy Cheddar Cheese Scones, page 13

Moroccan Bean Salad

Apricots, almonds and raisins add delicious sweet flavor to this intriguing bean salad.

Lemon Garlic Vinaigrette:

¼ cup	olive oil	60 mL
2 tbsp.	freshly squeezed lemon juice	30 mL
1 tsp.	sugar	5 mL
3	garlic cloves, crushed	3
1 tsp.	dried oregano	5 mL
½ tsp.	ground cumin	2 mL
½ tsp.	prepared mustard	2 mL
¼ tsp.	EACH salt and pepper	1 mL

19 oz.	can garbanzo beans, drained and rinsed	540 mL
19 oz.	can kidney beans, drained and rinsed	540 mL
19 oz.	can black beans, drained and rinsed	540 mL
¼ cup	chopped green onion	60 mL
½ cup	chopped dried apricots	125 mL
¼ cup	toasted whole almonds	60 mL
¼ cup	raisins, washed and dried	60 mL

Vinaigrette: In a small bowl, whisk together all vinaigrette ingredients until well blended; set aside.

In a large salad bowl, combine drained and rinsed beans, green onion, apricots, almonds and raisins; toss to combine. Whisk vinaigrette again and pour over salad; toss to combine. Cover and refrigerate for 2-4 hours. Stir before serving.

Serves 6-8

Bean Salad Fire and Ice Style

This make-ahead chilled marinated salad has spicy flavor and great texture.

19 oz.	can cut green beans, drained	454 g
19 oz.	can garbanzo beans, drained	454 g
19 oz.	can pinto beans, drained	454 g
1	large green OR red pepper, thinly sliced	1
1	red onion, thinly sliced	1

Spicy Vinaigrette:

½ cup	cider vinegar	125 mL
⅓ cup	olive oil	75 mL
1 tbsp.	sugar	15 mL
2	garlic cloves, minced	2
½ tsp.	crushed red pepper	2 mL
½ tsp.	chili powder	2 mL
¼ tsp.	ground cumin	1 mL
¼ tsp.	ground coriander	1 mL

In a large bowl, combine beans, peppers and onion; stir to combine.

Vinaigrette: In a shaker, or jar with a tight-fitting lid, combine vinegar, oil, sugar, garlic, crushed red pepper, chili powder, cumin and coriander. Cover jar tightly, shake vigorously.

Pour dressing over bean mixture; toss gently. Refrigerate in a tightly covered container for 8 hours, or overnight. Salad can be refrigerated for up to 2 days.

To serve, spoon into a serving bowl with a slotted spoon.

Serves 6-8

Pineapple and Vegetable Pasta Salad

Sweet pineapple and crisp chunky vegetables are perfect with this zesty dressing.

6 oz.	corkscrew pasta (approximately 1-1½ cups)	170 g
19 oz.	can pineapple chunks, drained and juice reserved	540 mL

Pineapple Dijon Dressing:

	reserved pineapple juice	
½ cup	olive oil	125 mL
¼ cup	white vinegar	60 mL
2 tsp.	Dijon mustard	10 mL
2 tsp.	Worcestershire sauce	10 mL
1	garlic clove, minced	1
⅛ tsp.	EACH salt and pepper	1 mL
1½ cups	cauliflower florets	375 mL
1½ cups	broccoli florets	375 mL
1 cup	seeded, chunked red pepper	250 mL
½ cup	chopped green onions	125 mL
½ cup	toasted whole almonds	125 mL

Cook pasta according to package directions; drain and set aside. Drain pineapple; reserve 2 tbsp. (30 mL) for dressing. Set aside.

Dressing: In a jar with a tight-fitting lid or a shaker, combine reserved pineapple juice, oil, vinegar, mustard, Worcestershire sauce, garlic, salt and pepper; shake well and set aside.

In a large salad bowl, combine cooked pasta, drained pineapple chunks, cauliflower, broccoli, red pepper, green onions and almonds. Shake dressing again, pour over salad and toss to coat. Cover and marinate in refrigerator for 4-6 hours. Taste and adjust seasonings just before serving.

Serves 6-8

Paella Salad

Enjoy the flavors of Spain by converting their ever popular paella into a main-dish salad that is oh-so-easy to make.

1 cup	chicken stock	250 mL
1 cup	quick-cooking rice	250 mL
¼ tsp.	ground turmeric	1 mL
1 lb.	cooked shrimp	500 g
1½ cups	frozen peas	375 mL
½ cup	chopped green onions	125 mL
⅓ cup	calorie-reduced Italian salad dressing (see page 80 or use a commercial dressing)	75 mL
⅛ tsp.	ground red pepper flakes OR cayenne pepper	0.5 mL
	tomato wedges for garnish	

In a small saucepan, heat chicken stock to boiling. Stir in rice and turmeric. Remove from heat; cover and allow to stand for 5 minutes, or until all liquid is absorbed. In a large salad bowl, combine shrimp, peas and onions. Add hot rice, salad dressing and red pepper to shrimp mixture; toss to coat well. Chill for several hours. Serve on lettuce-lined plates and garnish with tomatoes.

Serves 4-6

Turmeric has long been used in traditional Chinese and Indian medicine to treat many conditions, including menstrual cramps, angina, arthritis, flatulence, jaundice, colic, toothache, etc. The yellow pigment of turmeric (curcumin) has demonstrated potent anti-inflammatory properties with no toxicity. It also has very strong antioxidant effects which provides relief for rheumatoid arthritis and aids in cancer prevention. Recent studies have indicated that curcumin helps protect against Alzheimer's disease.

Shrimp and Oriental Vegetables with Creamy Horseradish Dressing

Serve as the main dish for a light summer meal.

Creamy Horseradish Dressing:

½ cup	low-fat mayonnaise	125 mL
¼ cup	low-fat plain yogurt	60 mL
3 tbsp.	lemon juice	45 mL
1 tbsp.	prepared horseradish	15 mL
2	garlic cloves, minced	2
1 lb.	cooked small shrimp	500 g
1 cup	snow peas	250 mL
8 oz.	can sliced water chestnuts, drained	227 mL
1 cup	sliced mushrooms	250 mL
1 cup	diagonally sliced celery	250 mL
1 cup	bean sprouts	250 mL
¼ cup	sliced green onions	60 mL
	shredded lettuce	

Dressing: In a small bowl, whisk together mayonnaise, yogurt, lemon juice, horseradish and garlic; set aside.

In a large salad bowl, combine shrimp, snow peas, water chestnuts, mushrooms, celery, bean sprouts and green onions; toss gently to combine. Stir dressing, pour over salad; toss gently to combine. Serve immediately over a bed of shredded lettuce.

Serves 4-6

Crab Salad with Creamy Dijon Dressing

The Dijon adds zest to this salad. A great summer main-dish meal.

Creamy Dijon Dressing:

½ cup	low-fat cottage cheese	125 mL
2 tbsp.	light sour cream	30 mL
2 tsp.	Dijon mustard	10 mL
1	garlic clove, minced	1
⅛ tsp.	pepper	0.5 mL
8 oz.	crabmeat or imitation crabmeat, chopped	250 g
¼ cup	chopped celery	60 mL
¼ cup	chopped green onion	60 mL
¼ cup	chopped cucumber	60 mL
	lettuce leaves	
1	tomato, cut into wedges	1

In a medium bowl, combine cottage cheese, sour cream, mustard, garlic and pepper; mix well.

Stir crabmeat, celery, onion and cucumber into dressing. Serve on lettuce-lined plates with tomato wedges.

Serves 2

 Garlic has many therapeutic benefits. Regular garlic consumption lowers blood pressure, decreases LDL (bad) cholesterol and boosts HDL (good) cholesterol. It helps prevent atherosclerosis and diabetic heart disease and reduces heart attack and stroke risk. Garlic is rich in several beneficial sulpher compounds, vitamins C and B_6, plus selenium and manganese. Both raw and cooked garlic increase anti-inflammatory, anti-bacterial and anti-viral activity in the body. Garlic is a potent antibiotic.

Peach and Chicken Salad with Orange Yogurt Dressing

The tangy dressing really brings this salad to life. A wonderful combination.

Orange Yogurt Dressing:

2 tbsp	unsweetened orange juice	30 mL
1 tbsp.	cider vinegar	15 mL
1 tbsp.	low-fat plain yogurt	15 mL
1 tsp.	grated orange zest	5 mL
1	garlic clove, minced	1
1 tsp.	sugar	5 mL
¼ tsp.	salt	1 mL
⅛ tsp.	pepper	0.5 mL
¼ cup	olive oil	60 mL
4 cups	torn fresh spinach	1 L
4 cups	torn lettuce	1 L
½ cup	chopped celery	125 mL
¼ cup	sliced green onions	60 mL
2	fresh peaches, peeled and sliced	2
2 cups	cubed, cooked chicken	500 mL

Dressing: In a blender or food processor, combine orange juice, vinegar, yogurt, orange zest, garlic, sugar, salt and pepper; process for 30 seconds. While processing, gradually add oil in a steady stream; process until sugar is dissolved and mixture is smooth.

In a large salad bowl, combine spinach, lettuce, celery, onions, peaches and chicken. Drizzle with dressing; toss to coat. Serve immediately.

Serves 6-8

Pictured on page 69.

Chicken, Grapefruit and Vegetable Salad

A wonderful main-dish salad that adapts nicely to any dressing.

4 cups	shredded lettuce	1 L
½ cup	chopped green onions	125 mL
1½ cups	cooked, diced chicken	375 mL
2	pink grapefruits, peeled and sectioned	2
2 cups	chopped tomatoes	500 mL
1 cup	sliced celery	250 mL

In a large salad bowl, combine all ingredients; toss to combine. Serve with your favorite salad dressing or Creamy Dill Yogurt Dressing, page 81 or French Dressing, page 82.

Serves 4

Grapefruit contains compounds which help to fight cold symptoms, prevent lung, colon and other cancers, plus stroke and heart disease. It is an excellent source of vitamin C, which helps reduce the severity of inflammatory conditions such as asthma, osteo and rheumatoid arthritis. Pink and red grapefruits contain lycopene which helps fight free radicals. Limonoids found in grapefruit help to inhibit tumor formation.

Caesar Salad with Grilled Turkey Breast

The all-time classic favorite with grilled turkey added – a full-meal dish.

Low-Fat Caesar Dressing:

5	garlic cloves, mashed	5
3 tbsp.	fresh lemon juice	45 mL
2 tbsp.	light sour cream OR low-fat plain yogurt	30 mL
1 tbsp.	olive oil	15 mL
½ tsp.	Worcestershire sauce	2 mL
¼ tsp.	dry mustard	1 mL
1 lb.	boneless, skinless turkey breast	500 g
¼ tsp.	salt	1 mL
¼ tsp.	pepper	1 mL
8 cups	romaine lettuce	2 L
¾ cup	croûtons	175 mL
¼ cup	grated Parmesan cheese	60 mL

Dressing: In a shaker or jar with a tight-fitting lid, combine mashed garlic, lemon juice, sour cream, oil, Worcestershire sauce and mustard; shake until well blended. Set aside.

Preheat grill to medium-hot. Sprinkle turkey with salt and pepper and lightly coat with nonstick cooking spray. Grill until cooked through, 10-15 minutes on each side. Remove turkey from grill and allow to set for 8-10 minutes. Slice turkey across grain ½" (1.3 cm) thick. In a large salad bowl, toss together romaine lettuce, croûtons and turkey. Sprinkle salad with Parmesan cheese. Shake dressing to mix; pour over salad and toss to combine or dressing can be served on the side.

Serves 4

Variations: Substitute grilled salmon or shrimp for the turkey.

Italian Herb Dressing

Wine vinegar adds rich flavor.

⅔ cup	olive oil	150 mL
⅓ cup	wine vinegar	75 mL
2	garlic cloves, minced	2
1 tsp.	dry mustard	5 mL
½ tsp.	salt	2 mL
½ tsp.	crushed dried basil	2 mL
½ tsp.	crushed dried oregano	2 mL
¼ tsp.	crushed red pepper	1 mL

In a jar with a tight-fitting lid or in a shaker, combine all ingredients; cover and shake vigorously. Chill to blend flavors. Shake again before serving over your favorite tossed green salads.

Makes 1 cup (250 mL)

Dill and Onion Vinaigrette

Zesty apple cider vinegar and dry mustard make this dressing special.

½ cup	olive oil	125 mL
⅓ cup	apple cider vinegar	75 mL
2 tbsp.	chopped green onion	30 mL
1 tsp.	dried dillweed	5 mL
½ tsp.	EACH salt and dry mustard	2 mL

In a jar with a tight-fitting lid or in a shaker, combine all ingredients; cover and shake vigorously. Chill to blend flavors. Shake again before serving over your favorite mixed vegetable salads.

Makes 1 cup (250 mL)

Lime Juice and Oil Dressing

This dressing is light and lively.

½ cup	lime juice	125 mL
4 tbsp.	olive oil	60 mL
3 tsp.	sugar	15 mL
1 tsp.	paprika	5 mL
½ tsp.	salt	2 mL
½ tsp.	dry mustard	2 mL

In a jar with a tight-fitting lid or in a shaker, combine all ingredients; cover and shake vigorously. Chill to blend flavors. Shake again before serving over your favorite mixed vegetable or tossed green salads.

Makes 1 cup (250 mL)

Creamy Dill Yogurt Dressing

The fresh flavor of dill enhances the tang of yogurt.

1 cup	low-fat plain yogurt	250 mL
½ tsp.	dried dillweed	2 mL
⅛ tsp.	hot pepper sauce	0.5 mL

In a small bowl, combine all ingredients; stir well to combine. Cover and refrigerate 2-4 hours.

Makes 1 cup (250 mL)

Pure, extra-virgin olive oil is one of the most health-promoting oils available. It is rich in monounsaturated fat, a type of fat that researchers are discovering has excellent health benefits. It has a powerful compound (oleocanthal) that may help decrease risk of stroke, heart disease, cancer and some dementias.

Walnut Dressing

A fabulous dressing for fruit salads.

1 cup	walnuts	250 mL
½ cup	olive oil	125 mL
4 tbsp.	lemon juice	60 mL
1	garlic clove	1

In a blender or food processor, combine all ingredients; blend or process until nuts are finely chopped. Refrigerate until well chilled. Serve over fruit or green salads.

Makes 1 cup (250 mL)

French Dressing

Now you can make this popular dressing at home.

½ cup	tomato ketchup	125 mL
½ cup	olive oil	125 mL
¼ cup	apple cider vinegar`	60 mL
1 tbsp.	icing (confectioner's) sugar	15 mL
1	garlic clove, minced	1
¼ tsp.	salt	1 mL
⅛ tsp.	pepper	0.5 mL

In a jar with a tight-fitting lid or in a shaker, combine all ingredients; cover and shake vigorously. Chill to blend flavors. Shake again before serving over your favorite mixed vegetable or tossed green salads.

Makes 1 cup (250 mL)

Vegetable Dishes

Stir-Fries
Roasted Vegetables
Potatoes
Rice

Five-Vegetable Stir-Fry with Dill

This is a great combination of vegetables — the water chestnuts add a nice crunch to the dish. Use fresh dill when in season.

1 tbsp.	olive oil	15 mL
2-3 tbsp.	chicken stock	30-45 mL
1½ cups	sliced mushrooms	375 mL
1 cup	diagonally sliced celery	250 mL
½ cup	chopped red peppers	125 mL
½ tsp.	dried dillweed	2 mL
2 cups	frozen peas	500 mL
¾ cup	sliced water chestnuts	175 mL

Heat oil in a large frying pan over medium heat. Stir in chicken stock, mushrooms, celery, red peppers and dillweed. Cook, stirring often, for about 6 minutes, or until vegetables are almost tender. Stir in peas and water chestnuts; cook, covered, for 2-3 minutes, stirring occasionally.

Serves 4-6

Dill has been a popular seasoning for thousands of years. It contains two types of healing components which give protection against free radicals and carcinogens. Its volatile oils can help neutralize carcinogens found in smoke and they also have bacteria-regulating effects. It is a very good source of calcium and a good source of manganese, iron and magnesium.

Stir-Fried Asparagus and Peas with Sesame Seeds

Sesame seeds add a lovely nutty flavor to this easy stir-fry.

2 tsp.	sesame seeds, toasted	10 mL
1 tbsp.	olive oil	15 mL
½ cup	chopped red onion	125 mL
2	garlic cloves, minced	2
1¼ lbs.	fresh asparagus, cut into 2" (5 cm) lengths	625 g
1 cup	frozen peas OR fresh snow peas	250 mL
½ tsp.	salt	2 mL

Toast sesame seeds in a small, heavy frying pan over low heat, stirring constantly until golden brown, about 3 minutes. Transfer to a plate to prevent further cooking; set aside.

Heat oil in a large frying pan over medium heat. Add onion and garlic, and cook, stirring constantly, until tender, about 5 minutes. Add asparagus, peas and salt to pan; cook, stirring frequently, until asparagus is crisp-tender and peas are heated through, about 5 minutes. Sprinkle sesame seeds over vegetables and toss to combine.

Serves 4

Tip: This recipe can be the basis for a pasta main dish. Cook 4 servings of any type of pasta, drain, and toss with the hot vegetables. Top with a dollop of fat-free sour cream for a special touch.

Pictured on the front cover.

Cauliflower and Asparagus Stir-Fry

This orange-flavored vegetable dish is a star performer for any meal. It will complement any menu, from broiled steak to roast chicken.

½ tsp.	grated orange zest	2 mL
⅓ cup	unsweetened orange juice	75 mL
1 tsp.	cornstarch	5 mL
¼ tsp.	ground ginger	1 mL
⅛ tsp.	salt	0.5 mL
1 tbsp.	olive oil	15 mL
1½ cups	thinly sliced cauliflower florets	375 mL
¾ lb.	fresh asparagus, cut into 2" (5 cm) pieces	340 g
2 tbsp.	slivered or sliced almonds, toasted orange slices for garnish (optional)	30 mL

In a small bowl, stir together orange zest, orange juice, cornstarch, ginger and salt; set aside. In a large frying pan or wok, heat oil over medium-high heat. Add cauliflower and stir-fry for 1 minute. Add asparagus and stir-fry about 3-4 minutes, or until vegetables are tender-crisp. Stir orange sauce mixture; add to center of the frying pan. Cook, stirring constantly, until sauce is thickened and bubbly and vegetables are coated, about 1 minute. Transfer vegetable mixture to a serving plate; sprinkle with toasted almonds. If desired, garnish with orange slices.

Serves 4

Oven-Roasted Squash and Asparagus

This is a nice combination of mild-flavored vegetables, a great side dish.

1	medium zucchini, sliced	1
1	medium summer squash, cut into 1" (2.5 cm) cubes	1
1	red pepper, thickly sliced	1
1 lb.	fresh asparagus, cut into 1" (2.5 cm) lengths	500 g
1	sliced red onion	1
1 tbsp.	olive oil	15 mL
½ tsp.	salt	2 mL
¼ tsp.	pepper	1 mL

Preheat oven to 375°F (190°C). Combine zucchini, squash, red pepper, asparagus and onion in a 10 x 15" (25 x 38 cm) baking pan or a small roasting pan; toss with oil, salt and pepper. Roast for 50-60 minutes, stirring occasionally, or until vegetables are lightly browned and tender.

Serves 4-6

Summer squash varieties include zucchini, crookneck and straightneck squash, pattypan squash and vegetable marrow (marrow squash). The flesh, skin and seeds are all edible. Summer squash have some cancer-preventative effects and may promote prostate health. They also provide well-rounded cardiovascular protection as they are an excellent source of manganese and vitamin C, plus a very good source of magnesium, vitamin A, fiber, potassium, folate, copper, riboflavin and phosphorus.

Grilled Zucchini and Squash Kabobs

These colorful kabobs are great for a summer barbecue.

1	medium yellow summer squash	1
1	medium zucchini	1
1	red pepper	1

Lemon Herb Marinade:

4-6 tbsp.	olive oil	60-90 mL
2 tsp.	grated lemon zest	10 mL
1 tsp.	wine vinegar	5 mL
¼ cup	fresh lemon juice	60 mL
3	garlic cloves, minced	3
2 tsp.	dried basil	10 mL
1 tsp.	dried oregano	5 mL
1 tsp.	dried savory	5 mL
1 tsp.	pepper	5 mL

Wash vegetables thoroughly; cut into 1" (2.5 cm) pieces. Place vegetables in a 9 x 13" (23 x 33 cm) baking dish.

Marinade: In a shaker or a jar with a tight-fitting lid, combine all marinade ingredients. Cover tightly and shake vigorously.

Pour marinade over vegetables. Cover and refrigerate for up to 24 hours. Remove vegetables from marinade. Alternate vegetables on four, 5" (13 cm) skewers. Grill vegetables over hot coals for 8-10 minutes, or until tender, turning once and basting frequently with marinade.

Serves 2

Tomato Zucchini Casserole

A very tasty side dish – zucchini and vegetables cooked in a tomato sauce and accented with mozzarella cheese, this can also double as a main dish by just adding a salad.

4 cups	sliced zucchini	1 L
1 cup	sliced green OR red peppers	250 mL
½ cup	chopped celery	125 mL
1 cup	sliced onions	250 mL
8 oz.	can tomato sauce	227 mL
2 cups	shredded low-fat mozzarella cheese	500 mL

Preheat oven to 375°F (190°C). Layer vegetables in a 10" (25 cm) casserole or baking dish. Pour tomato sauce over vegetables. Cover and bake for 30 minutes, or until vegetables are tender. Remove cover and sprinkle with cheese. Continue to bake until cheese is melted and lightly browned.

Serves 4-6

Zucchini & Carrot Sauté

Quick, easy, good for you and very tasty.

1 tbsp.	olive oil	15 mL
1 lb.	thinly sliced carrots	500 g
1	onion, sliced and separated into rings	1
2	small zucchini, sliced	2
2 tsp.	dried basil	10 mL
¼ tsp.	salt	1 mL
⅛ tsp.	pepper	0.5 mL

In a large frying pan, heat oil over medium heat. Add carrots and sauté for 4-5 minutes. Add onion; cook for 1 minute. Stir in zucchini, basil, salt and pepper. Cover and cook for 4-5 minutes, or until vegetables are tender-crisp. Serve immediately.

Serves 4

Pineapple and Ginger-Glazed Baby Carrots

Ginger adds spicy flavor to carrots.

1½ lbs.	baby carrots	750 g
⅔ cup	unsweetened pineapple juice	150 mL
2 tsp.	cornstarch	10 mL
¼ tsp.	ground ginger OR ground nutmeg	1 mL

In a medium saucepan, boil carrots over medium heat for 10-15 minutes, or until tender-crisp. Drain; cover to keep warm. In a small saucepan, combine pineapple juice, cornstarch and ginger. Cook over medium heat, stirring constantly, until thickened and bubbly, about 2-3 minutes. Pour glaze over carrots; stir to coat. Serve immediately.

Serves 4

Sweet and Sour Red Cabbage

This tangy side dish goes wonderfully well with pork.

1 tbsp.	olive oil	15 mL
¾ cup	chopped onion	175 mL
1	green OR red pepper, thinly sliced	1
1	small head red cabbage	1
2	apples, cored, thinly sliced	2
¼ cup	cider vinegar	60 mL
3 tbsp.	brown sugar	45 mL
½ tsp.	salt	2 mL
¼ tsp.	pepper	1 mL

Heat oil in a large frying pan over medium heat. Add onion and pepper; cook until soft, about 3 minutes. Stir in cabbage; cover and cook for 5 minutes. Add apples, vinegar, sugar, salt and pepper; stir well to combine. Cover and cook for 10-15 minutes, or until cabbage is tender. If necessary, a little water may be added to prevent sticking. Serve immediately.

Serves 4-6

Lemon Broccoli Sauté

Lemon truly enhances the flavor of broccoli. This great side dish can be served with any meal.

1	large bunch broccoli, cut into spears	1
1 tbsp.	olive oil	15 mL
1	thinly sliced onion	1
1 cup	thinly sliced celery	250 mL
3	garlic cloves, minced	3
2 tsp.	grated lemon zest	10 mL
1½ tsp.	lemon juice	7 mL
¼ tsp.	salt	1 mL
⅛ tsp.	pepper	0.5 mL

Place broccoli in a steaming basket over 1" (2.5 cm) of boiling water in a saucepan. Cover and steam for 5-6 minutes, or until tender-crisp. Drain and rinse under cold water; set aside. In a large frying pan over medium heat, heat oil and sauté onion, celery and garlic until vegetables are tender, about 5 minutes. Add lemon zest, lemon juice, salt, pepper and broccoli; stir to combine; cook for an additional 2-3 minutes. Serve immediately.

Serves 4

Pictured on page 121.

Lemons contain phytonutrients that have antioxidant, anti-cancer and antibiotic properties. An excellent source of vitamin A, they are helpful in reducing some of the symptoms of osteo and rheumatoid arthritis and are important in maintaining a strong immune system. Limonoids compounds in lemons have been shown to help fight mouth, skin, lung, breast, stomach and colon cancers, and protect against macular degeneration.

Broccoli with Almonds

The almonds provide a bit of a crunch to this great side dish. Serve with any menu.

1½ lbs.	broccoli, cut into spears	750 g
1 cup	chicken stock	250 mL
¼ cup	sliced almonds	60 mL
1 tbsp.	olive oil	15 mL
½ cup	chopped red onion	125 mL
½ cup	chopped celery	125 mL

In a large saucepan, bring broccoli and chicken stock to a boil. Reduce heat; cover, and simmer for 5-8 minutes, or until broccoli is tender-crisp. Drain; cover to keep warm; set aside. In a small frying pan over medium heat, stirring constantly, sauté almonds in oil until nicely browned. Add onion and celery; sauté until tender. Transfer broccoli to a serving dish; spoon sautéed almond mixture over and toss to coat. Serve immediately.

Serves 6

Parmesan Brussels Sprouts

An easy and quick way to zest up a basic side dish.

1 lb.	Brussels sprouts	500 g
2	garlic cloves, minced	2
2 tbsp.	grated Parmesan cheese	30 mL

Place Brussels sprouts and garlic in a medium saucepan; add approximately 1" (2.5 cm) of water. Bring to a boil; reduce heat. Cover and simmer for 6-8 minutes, or until the sprouts are tender-crisp; drain. Transfer to a serving bowl and immediately sprinkle with Parmesan. Toss slightly to distribute and allow cheese to melt slightly.

Serves 4

Roasted Root Vegetables with Brussels Sprouts

A unique and delicious side dish for a harvest-time meal. This dish has become a favorite of our family for Thanksgiving dinner.

1 lb.	small potatoes, unpeeled, cut in half	500 g
3	carrots, cut into ½" (1.3 cm) slices	3
2	parsnips, cut into ½" (1.3 cm) slices	2
1	small turnip, peeled, cut into ½" (1.3 cm) cubes	1
1	onion, cut into ½" (1.3 cm) wedges	1
1 tbsp.	olive oil	15 mL
1 tsp.	dried thyme	5 mL
½ tsp.	salt	2 mL
¼ tsp.	pepper	1 mL
1½ cups	Brussels sprouts, halved	375 mL
2	garlic cloves, quartered	2

Preheat oven to 375°F (190°C). In a roasting pan or 10 x 15" (25 x 38 cm) baking pan, combine potatoes, carrots, parsnips, turnip and onion. In a small bowl, combine oil, thyme, salt and pepper; drizzle over vegetables and toss to coat. Cover and bake for 30 minutes. Add Brussels sprouts and garlic; bake, uncovered, for an additional 30 minutes, or until vegetables are tender, stirring every 10 minutes. Serve immediately.

Serves 8-10

Stuffed Baked Sweet Potatoes

Apricot nectar and orange zest are wonderful flavor partners with these succulent sweet potatoes.

4	medium sweet potatoes	4
½ cup	apricot nectar	125 mL
¼ cup	low-fat milk	60 mL
2 tsp.	butter OR margarine, melted	10 mL
1 tsp.	grated orange zest	5 mL
¼ tsp.	EACH salt and ground nutmeg	1 mL
¼-½ cup	finely chopped pecans, toasted	60-125 mL

Preheat oven to 400°F (200°C). Scrub sweet potatoes; pat dry. Prick each potato several times with a fork. Arrange on a baking sheet. Bake for 1 hour, or until tender. Allow potatoes to cool to touch. Cut a 1" (2.5 cm) lengthwise strip from top of each potato; carefully scoop out pulp, leaving shell intact. In a medium bowl, combine potato pulp, apricot nectar, milk, melted butter, orange zest, salt and nutmeg. With an electric mixer, beat at medium speed until light and fluffy. Stir in pecans. Spoon mixture evenly back into potato shells; place shells back on baking sheet and bake for 15-20 minutes, or until heated through. To make-ahead, refrigerate stuffed potatoes in a tightly covered container for up to 24 hours. Bake as above for 25-30 minutes.

Serves 4

Oven-Roasted Sweet Potatoes

Sweet and spicy – serve these potatoes with pork or chicken.

3	large sweet potatoes, peeled and cut into 1" (2.5 cm) cubes	3
1 tbsp.	olive oil	15 mL
2 tbsp.	brown sugar	30 mL
1 tsp.	chili powder	5 mL
½ tsp.	salt	2 mL
¼ tsp.	cayenne pepper	1 mL

Oven-Roasted Sweet Potatoes Continued

Preheat oven to 400°F (200°C). Place potato cubes in a 9 x 13" (23 x 33 cm) baking pan. Add oil; toss to coat well. In a small bowl, combine brown sugar, chili powder, salt and cayenne pepper. Sprinkle over potatoes in pan; toss to coat well. Bake, uncovered, for 40-45 minutes, or until potatoes are tender, stirring every 10-15 minutes.

Serves 6-8

Variations: To make **Oven-Roasted Potato Wedges**, cut white or sweet potatoes into long wedges. Toss with just enough olive oil to coat and sprinkle with salt, pepper and chili powder to taste. For **Herbed Baked Potato Wedges**, omit chili powder, oil wedges and sprinkle with Italian Herbs. Bake as above.

Scalloped Potatoes

A lighter version of an old favorite.

Creamy Sauce:

1 cup	skim milk	250 mL
2 tsp.	cornstarch	10 mL
¼ tsp.	salt	1 mL
¼ tsp.	pepper	1 mL
2	large potatoes	2
¼ cup	chopped onion	60 mL
2 tbsp.	grated Parmesan cheese	30 mL

Preheat oven to 350°F (180°C).

Sauce: In a small saucepan, stir together milk, cornstarch, salt and pepper. Place over medium heat; stirring constantly, cook until thickened and bubbly, about 2-3 minutes. Remove from heat; set aside.

Lightly spray a 1½-quart (1.5 L) casserole with nonstick spray coating. Peel potatoes and slice very thinly. Layer half of the potatoes and half of the onions into the casserole. Repeat potato and onion layers. Pour sauce over potato mixture; sprinkle with Parmesan cheese. Bake, covered, for 40 minutes. Uncover and bake for an additional 10-15 minutes, or until potatoes are tender. Serve immediately.

Serves 4

Soybeans in Sweet and Sour Sauce

This recipe was given to us by a close friend who grows soybeans. It is a wonderful meatless dish packed full of protein.

1 tbsp.	olive oil	15 mL
3	garlic cloves, minced	3
1	large onion, cut into wedges	1
½ cup	celery, sliced diagonally	125 mL
1 cup	red OR green peppers, cut into strips	250 mL
½ cup	carrots, sliced diagonally	125 mL
1 cup	broccoli florets	250 mL
2 cups	cooked soybeans	500 mL
19 oz.	pineapple chunks, drained	540 mL

Sweet & Sour Sauce:

1 tbsp.	cornstarch	15 mL
¼ tsp.	ground ginger	1 mL
2 tbsp.	soy sauce	30 mL
¼ cup	vinegar	60 mL
½ cup	unsweetened pineapple juice	125 mL

Soybean Preparation: Soak ¾ cup (175 mL) soybeans in 3 cups (750 mL) of cold water in the refrigerator overnight, or for 8-10 hours. Drain and place in a medium-sized saucepan; add 3 cups (750 mL) of cold water. Place over high heat and bring to a boil; reduce heat and simmer for 2 hours.

In a wok or large frying pan, heat oil over medium-high heat. Add garlic, onion, celery, peppers, carrots and broccoli; stir-fry until vegetables are tender-crisp, about 3-4 minutes. Add soybeans and pineapple chunks; continue to stir-fry for 2-3 minutes.

Sauce: In a small bowl, combine all sauce ingredients; pour over vegetable mixture and cook until sauce boils and thickens, about 2-3 minutes. Serve immediately over brown rice. Garnish with sesame seeds, cashews or peanuts.

Serves 6

Nutty Rice

2 cups	water	250 mL
2 tsp.	butter OR margarine	10 mL
½ tsp.	salt	2 mL
1 cup	uncooked long-grain rice	250 mL
1 cup	finely chopped pecans OR walnuts, toasted	250 mL
½ cup	frozen peas, thawed	125 mL

In a medium saucepan, combine water, butter and salt; set over medium heat and bring to a boil. Add rice; cover, reduce heat to low and simmer for 20 minutes, or until rice is tender and water is absorbed. Remove from heat. Gently stir in pecans and peas. Serve immediately.

Serves 4

Spanish Rice

An old favorite – a little bit hot and spicy.

1 tbsp.	olive oil	15 mL
½ cup	chopped onion	125 mL
½ cup	chopped green OR red pepper	125 mL
1	garlic clove, minced	1
28 oz.	can tomatoes with juice	796 mL
2 cups	cooked brown rice	500 mL
1 tsp.	sugar	5 mL
1 tsp.	chili powder	5 mL
⅛ tsp.	pepper	0.5 mL
⅛ tsp.	hot pepper sauce	0.5 mL
½ cup	shredded low-fat Cheddar cheese	125 mL

In a large frying pan, heat oil over medium heat; add onion, peppers and garlic. Cook and stir until onion is tender. Stir in tomatoes with liquid, cooked rice, sugar, chili powder, pepper and hot pepper sauce; bring to a boil. Reduce heat; cover and simmer for 15-20 minutes, or until heated through. Sprinkle with cheese. Serve immediately.

Serves 4

Oriental-Style Rice Pilaf

1 tbsp.	olive oil	15 mL
½ cup	chopped onion	125 mL
2	garlic cloves, minced	2
1¾ cups	beef stock	425 mL
1 cup	uncooked long-grain rice	250 mL
1 tbsp.	soy sauce	15 mL
¼ tsp.	crushed red pepper flakes	1 mL
½ cup	sliced green onions	125 mL
⅓ cup	diced red pepper	75 mL
2 tbsp.	toasted sesame seeds	30 mL

In a medium-sized saucepan, heat oil over medium heat, cook onion and garlic until onion is tender. Add beef stock, rice, soy sauce and pepper flakes. Bring to a boil; stir once or twice. Reduce heat; cover and simmer for 15-20 minutes, or until rice is tender and liquid is absorbed. Stir green onions and red pepper into cooked rice; cover and allow to stand 5 minutes. Fluff with a fork. Transfer to a serving bowl and sprinkle with sesame seeds. Serve immediately.

Serves 4-6

Rice and Noodle Pilaf

Browned and then cooked in chicken stock, this dish has great flavor.

2 tsp.	butter OR margarine	10 mL
1 cup	long-grain rice	250 mL
½ cup	fine egg noodles	125 mL
2¾ cups	chicken stock	675 mL
2 tbsp.	minced fresh parsley	30 mL

In a medium-sized saucepan, melt butter over medium heat. Add rice and noodles; cook and stir until lightly browned, about 3 minutes. Stir in stock; bring to a boil. Reduce heat; cover and simmer for 20-25 minutes, or until stock is absorbed and rice is tender. Stir in parsley.

Serves 4

Pictured on page 121.

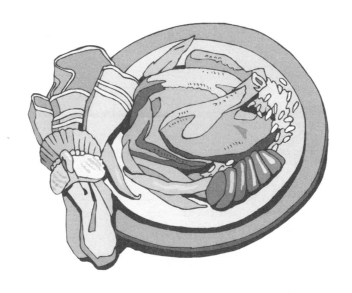

Main Course Dishes

Eggs, Beans & Pasta
Seafood
Poultry
Pork
Beef

Mushroom and Red Pepper Frittata

Eggs were once just a breakfast and brunch dish. Served with a fresh, crisp salad, egg dishes such as this one are a substantial main dish. Substitute or add your favorite veggies.

1 tbsp.	olive oil	15 mL
½ cup	chopped onion	125 mL
1	garlic clove, minced	1
¼ cup	diced red pepper	60 mL
2 cups	sliced mushrooms	500 mL
6	eggs	6
½ tsp.	salt	2 mL
⅛ tsp.	cayenne pepper	0.5 mL
¾ cup	low-fat mozzarella cheese	175 mL
2 tbsp.	chopped fresh parsley	30 mL

In a large frying pan, heat oil over medium heat; add onions, garlic, red pepper and mushrooms. Sauté together until vegetables are tender and moisture has evaporated, about 5-6 minutes. Whisk eggs together with salt and pepper. Stir in mozzarella and parsley. Pour egg mixture gently over vegetable mixture in pan. Increase heat to medium-high. Cook until bottom sets, lifting frittata with a spatula to allow uncooked eggs to flow underneath and set. When edges are firm but top is still moist, cover frying pan with a large plate; turn over together so frittata is cooked side up on the plate and slide frittata back into skillet, cooked side up. Cook 1-2 minutes longer or until bottom is set. Cook just until set. OR, if you have an ovenproof frying pan, you may finish cooking the top of the frittata under a preheated broiler. Transfer frittata to a serving dish and cut into wedges.

Serves 4

Pictured on page 103.

Six-Vegetable Quiche

¼ cup	whole-wheat bread crumbs	60 mL
1 tsp.	olive oil	5 mL
1 cup	EACH sliced zucchini and mushrooms	250 mL
½ cup	chopped onion	125 mL
½ cup	frozen corn	125 mL
½ cup	EACH chopped red and green pepper	125 mL
¼ tsp.	EACH dried basil and oregano	1 mL
¼ tsp.	salt	1 mL
⅛ tsp.	pepper	0.5 mL
¾ cup	low-fat cottage cheese, drained	175 mL
4	eggs, beaten	4
⅔ cup	low-fat evaporated milk	150 mL
3 tbsp.	freshly grated Parmesan cheese	45 mL

Preheat oven to 350°F (180°C). Spray a 9" (23 cm) quiche pan or pie plate with nonstick spray. Sprinkle with bread crumbs. In a large frying pan, heat oil over medium-high heat. Add zucchini, mushrooms, onion, corn and peppers; cook for 6-8 minutes, or until softened and no longer moist, stirring occasionally. Stir in basil, oregano, salt and pepper. Spoon vegetables into the prepared pan. Spoon the cottage cheese over the vegetables. In a large bowl with an electric mixer, beat eggs until light; whisk in milk and pour over the cottage cheese and vegetables. Sprinkle with Parmesan cheese. Bake for 45-60 minutes, or until puffy and set in the center. Let stand for 5 minutes before cutting.

Serves 6

Eggs are a good source of high-quality protein with a caloric cost of only 68 calories per egg. In fact, egg protein is used as the standard in measuring other protein foods. Eggs provide a source of choline, an essential nutrient for good healthy brain and nervous system functioning. The egg white is mainly protein and the yolk provides 11 essential vitamins and minerals. The lutein in eggs contributes to eye health. Recent studies have shown that eggs do not have a negative effect on blood cholesterol levels.

Vegetable and Fettuccini Toss

A pasta dish that is light and tasty.

1 cup	fettuccini, cooked as package directions	250 mL
1 tbsp.	olive oil	15 mL
½ cup	chopped onion	125 mL
1	garlic clove, minced	1
1 tsp.	Italian seasoning	5 mL
¼ cup	beef stock	60 mL
2 cups	broccoli florets	500 mL
2 cups	sliced zucchini	500 mL
2 cups	sliced mushrooms	500 mL
1	small red pepper, cut into strips	1
1	small green pepper, cut into strips	1
¼ cup	grated Parmesan cheese	60 mL

Cook fettuccini according to package directions; drain and keep warm. In a large frying pan, heat oil over medium heat; add onion, garlic and Italian seasoning. Cook, stirring constantly, until onion is tender. Add beef stock, broccoli, zucchini, mushrooms, red and green peppers; cover and simmer for 5-7 minutes, or until vegetables are tender-crisp. Toss with hot fettuccini; sprinkle with Parmesan cheese.

Serves 4

Onions, like garlic, are rich in sulpher compounds and also in chromium, vitamin C and many flavenoids. Onions help to lower blood-sugar levels, high cholesterol levels and high blood pressure. Colon cancer prevention, boosting bone health, as well as anti-inflammatory and anti-bacterial properties make onions a valuable nutrition source. Add onions and garlic to soups and stews during cold and flu season. See recipe on page 40.

Vegetarian Main Course

Mushroom and Red Pepper Frittata, page 100
Toasted Pistachio and Romaine Salad with Cranberry Vinaigrette, page 57

Herbed Spinach-Stuffed Manicotti

A wonderful spinach and pasta dish baked in a herbed tomato sauce.

8	manicotti shells, cooked, rinsed and drained	8
1 tsp.	dried rosemary	5 mL
1 tsp.	dried oregano	5 mL
1 tsp.	dried thyme	5 mL
2	garlic cloves, minced	2
1 tsp.	olive oil	5 mL
1½ cups	fresh tomatoes, chopped	375 mL
10 oz.	package frozen spinach, cooked, drained, squeezed dry	283 g
½ cup	ricotta cheese	125 mL
2	egg whites, lightly beaten	2

Preheat oven to 350°F (180°C). Cook manicotti shells according to package directions; rinse, drain and set aside. In a small saucepan over medium heat, combine rosemary, oregano, thyme, garlic and olive oil. Cook, stirring constantly, for about 1 minute, do not let herbs brown. Add tomatoes, reduce heat to low and, stirring occasionally, simmer for 10 minutes; set aside. In a medium bowl, combine spinach and ricotta cheese; fold in egg whites. Stuff manicotti with spinach mixture. Place ⅓ of the tomato sauce on the bottom of a lightly buttered 9 x 13" (23 x 33 cm) baking pan. Arrange stuffed manicotti in pan. Pour remaining tomato sauce over manicotti. Cover with foil; bake for 30 minutes, or until bubbly. Serve immediately.

Serves 4

Vegetarian Lasagne

8-10	lasagne noodles, cooked as directed on package, rinsed, drained	8-10
19 oz.	can tomatoes with juice	540 mL
14 oz.	can tomato sauce	398 mL
1 tsp.	EACH dried oregano and basil	5 mL
⅛ tsp.	pepper	0.5 mL
1 tbsp.	olive oil	15 mL
1	chopped onion	1
2	garlic cloves, minced	2
2	small zucchini, chopped	2
2 cups	sliced mushrooms	500 mL
1	large carrot, chopped	1
1	green OR red pepper, chopped	1
2	eggs, lightly beaten	2
2 cups	low-fat cottage cheese	500 mL
⅔ cup	grated Parmesan cheese	150 mL
2 tsp.	olive oil	10 mL
1 tsp.	salt	5 mL
8 oz.	low-fat mozzarella cheese, sliced	250 g

Preheat oven to 350°F (180°C). Cook lasagne noodles according to package directions; rinse in cold water, drain and set aside.

In a small saucepan, combine tomatoes with juice, tomato sauce, oregano, basil and pepper. Place over low heat; simmer for 20-30 minutes. In a large frying pan, heat 1 tbsp. (15 mL) olive oil over medium-high heat; add onion and garlic. Cook, stirring constantly, until onion is tender. Add zucchini, mushrooms, carrot and peppers. Cook and stir until vegetables are tender-crisp, 4-6 minutes. Stir tomato sauce into vegetables; reduce heat and simmer 10-20 minutes. In a small bowl, combine eggs, cottage cheese, Parmesan cheese, 2 tsp. (10 mL) olive oil and salt; stir well.

Vegetarian Lasagne Continued

To assemble, pour half the vegetables into a lightly buttered 9 x 13" (23 x 33 cm) baking dish; top with half the cooked lasagne noodles; cover with the cottage cheese mixture; top with the remaining cooked lasagne noodles; pour the remaining vegetables over. Top with cheese slices. Bake for 45-60 minutes. Remove from the oven and allow to stand for 5-10 minutes before serving.

Serves 8-10

Note: Other vegetables may be added or substituted for those listed.

Noodles Romanoff

Macaroni and cheese never tasted so good!

8 oz.	curly egg noodles, cooked as package directions	250 g
1 cup	low-fat cottage cheese	250 mL
1 cup	light sour cream	250 mL
½ cup	sliced kalamata olives	125 mL
½ cup	sliced green onions	125 mL
1 tsp.	Worcestershire sauce	5 mL
½ tsp.	salt	2 mL
¼ tsp.	hot pepper sauce	1 mL
½ cup	shredded low-fat Cheddar cheese	125 mL

Preheat oven to 350°F (180°C). Cook noodles according to package directions, omitting salt. Drain well. Combine noodles, cottage cheese, sour cream, olives, green onions, Worcestershire sauce, salt and hot pepper sauce. Spoon noodles into a lightly buttered 7 x 11" (18 x 28 cm) baking dish; bake for 30-35 minutes. Remove from oven; sprinkle with Cheddar cheese. Bake an additional 5-8 minutes, or until cheese melts.

Serves 6-8

Pasta and Beans

Beans and pasta in a tomato-garlic sauce make a protein-packed vegetarian main dish.

1 tbsp.	olive oil	15 mL
1	carrot, thinly sliced	1
4	garlic cloves, minced	4
1 cup	tomato juice	250 mL
½ tsp.	salt	2 mL
19 oz.	can white beans, drained	540 mL
12 oz.	spinach penne, cooked as package directions	340 g
⅛ tsp.	pepper	0.5 mL
4 oz.	low-fat mozzarella cheese, cubed	115 g

Heat oil in a large frying pan over low heat. Add carrots and garlic; cook, stirring frequently, until carrot is tender, about 5 minutes. Stir in tomato juice and salt and bring to a boil. Add ¾ of the white beans; stir to combine and remove from heat; set aside. Place the remaining ¼ of the white beans in a small bowl and mash with a potato masher; stir into the vegetable mixture. Cook pasta in a large pot of boiling water according to package directions. Drain; reserving ½ cup (125 mL) of pasta cooking liquid. Transfer hot pasta to a large bowl. Add reserved pasta cooking liquid to the vegetable mixture. Reheat vegetables to boiling and pour over pasta in bowl; add pepper and toss to combine. Add mozzarella cubes and toss well. Serve immediately.

Serves 4

Spanish-Style Garbanzo Beans

A mild, tasty combination of garbanzo beans and corn, with a hint of oregano and garlic, all simmered with juicy tomatoes.

1 cup	dried garbanzo beans (chickpeas)	250 mL
2½ cups	cold water	625 mL
1 tsp.	salt	5 mL
1 tbsp.	olive oil	15 mL
½ cup	chopped onion	125 mL
3	garlic cloves, minced	3
28 oz.	can tomatoes with juice	796 mL
1½ cups	kernel corn	375 mL
¼-½ tsp.	oregano	1-2 mL

Bean Preparation: Sort, rinse and soak beans in 4-6 cups (1-1.5 L) cold water for 8-10 hours, or overnight. Drain beans and place in a large saucepan; add the 2½ cups (625 mL) cold water and salt. Place over medium-high heat and bring to a boil. Reduce heat and simmer until tender, about 1½-2 hours. Drain beans and return to saucepan; set aside.

In a small frying pan, heat oil and sauté onion and garlic until tender, about 3-4 minutes; add to drained beans in saucepan. Add tomatoes, corn and oregano to beans. Cover and simmer for 20-30 minutes. Serve immediately. This dish can be frozen and it reheats well.

Serves 4-6

Note: If you don't have the time or inclination to soak dried beans, sub-stitute a 19 oz. (540 mL) can of garbanzo beans. Drain and rinse well.

Foods rich in fiber, such as corn, which is a whole grain, lower cholesterol levels, reduce the risk of colon cancer, alleviate symptoms of irritable bowel syndrome and help to stabilize blood sugar levels. Beta-cryptoxanthin, found in corn, significantly lowers the risk of developing lung cancer and thiamin (Vitamin B₁) is critical for brain function and energy production. Yellow corn is also rich in carotenoids which may help keep your eyes healthy.

Sweet Potato Garbanzo Stew

This spicy high-energy stew makes a delicious winter pick-me-up main course.

1½ cups	pearled barley OR brown rice	375 mL
1 tbsp.	olive oil	15 mL
3	garlic cloves, minced	3
2	red peppers, cut into 1" (2.5 cm) chunks	2
1	large onion, chopped	1
1 tbsp.	minced fresh ginger	15 mL
½ tsp.	ground allspice	2 mL
½ tsp.	ground cumin	2 mL
½-1 tsp.	red pepper flakes	2-4 mL
4 cups	chicken OR vegetable stock	1 L
2	large sweet potatoes, peeled and cut into 1" (2.5 cm) chunks	2
½ cup	smooth peanut butter	125 mL
⅓ cup	tomato paste	75 mL
1 cup	boiling water	250 mL
19 oz.	chickpeas, rinsed and drained	540 mL
1 lb.	spinach, coarsely chopped	500 g

Prepare barley as package directions. Heat oil in a large saucepan over medium-high heat. Add garlic, peppers and onion. Cook for 3 minutes. Add ginger, allspice, cumin and red pepper flakes. Cook for 1 minute. Add stock and sweet potatoes and bring to a boil. Reduce heat to low, cover and simmer for 15 minutes.

In a bowl, whisk peanut butter and tomato paste with water. Stir into the stew. Add the chickpeas and spinach and cook for 10 minutes, or until heated through. Serve over barley.

Serves 6

 A sweet source of good nutrition, sweet potatoes are a rich antioxidant and anti-inflammatory food. They are an excellent source of vitamin A, in the form of beta-carotene, and a very good source of vitamin C.

Greek Vegetarian Pizza

A quick and easy supper or lunch dish.

6	whole-wheat pita bread rounds	6
1 cup	tomato sauce	250 mL
2 tbsp.	Italian seasoning	30 mL
1	garlic clove, minced	1
15	large mushrooms, thinly sliced	15
1 cup	diced tomatoes	250 mL
1	chopped green OR red pepper	1
½ cup	sliced kalamata olives	125 mL
1	small onion, chopped	1
½ cup	crumbled feta cheese	125 mL
2 cups	shredded low-fat mozzarella cheese	500 mL

Preheat oven to 400°F (200°C). Flatten pitas. In a small bowl, combine tomato sauce, Italian seasoning and garlic; spread over pitas. Top each pita with mushrooms, tomatoes, peppers, olives, onion and feta cheese. Sprinkle with mozzarella cheese. Place pitas on baking sheets and bake for 10-15 minutes. To serve, cut into triangles.

Serves 6

Low-fat varieties are available for many cheeses. Mozzarella cheese is a very good source of calcium and protein and a good source of selenium (cancer protection) and iodine (promotes healthy thyroid function). Calcium has been shown to help protect against colon cancer, help prevent bone loss, migraine headaches and reduce PMS symptoms. A recent medical study confirmed that eating more dairy products actually decreases the risk of gout.

Scallops and Tomatoes in Wine Sauce

This mild, delicately flavored dish is attractive on a bed of pasta or rice.

1 lb.	sea scallops	500 g
4 tsp.	cornstarch, divided	20 mL
2 tsp.	olive oil	10 mL
3	garlic cloves, minced	3
2 cups	cherry tomatoes	500 mL
½ cup	chopped celery	125 mL
⅔ cup	white wine OR chicken broth	150 mL
½ tsp.	salt	2 mL
⅓ cup	chopped fresh basil	75 mL
1 tbsp.	cold water	15 mL

Dredge scallops in 3 tsp. (15 mL) cornstarch, shaking off excess. Heat oil in a large frying pan over medium heat. Add scallops and sauté until golden brown and cooked through, about 3 minutes. With a slotted spoon, transfer scallops to a bowl. Add garlic to the pan and cook for 1 minute. Add tomatoes and celery; cook until tomatoes begin to collapse, about 4 minutes. Add wine or chicken broth, salt and basil to pan. Bring to a boil and cook for 1 minute. In a small bowl, stir together remaining 1 tsp. (5 mL) cornstarch and cold water. Add cornstarch mixture to pan and cook, stirring constantly, until sauce is slightly thickened, about 1 minute. Return scallops to pan, reduce heat to low and simmer until heated through, about 2-3 minutes. Serve with vermicelli or brown rice.

Serves 4

Shrimp Creole

A combination of shrimp and vegetables in a tangy tomato wine sauce

1 tbsp.	olive oil	15 mL
1½ lbs.	cooked shrimp	750 g
1	green OR red pepper, seeded, cut into strips	1
1	medium onion, peeled and sliced	1
1 cup	diagonally sliced celery	250 mL
2	garlic cloves, minced	2
2	medium tomatoes, cut into eighths	2
½ cup	white wine OR vegetable stock	125 mL
½ cup	tomato sauce	125 mL
1 tbsp.	prepared horseradish	15 mL
6-8 drops	hot pepper sauce	6-8 drops

In a large frying pan, heat oil over medium-high heat; add shrimp and cook for 3-4 minutes, or until browned. With a slotted spoon, transfer shrimp to a bowl and set aside. Add peppers, onion, celery and garlic to the frying pan; reduce heat to medium-low and sauté vegetables for 5-8 minutes, until tender-crisp. Add tomatoes and wine or vegetable stock and cook for 2 minutes on medium heat. Add tomato sauce, horseradish, hot pepper sauce and browned shrimp; stir to combine and continue to cook over medium heat until heated through, about 5-8 minutes. Serve immediately over rice.

Serves 4-6

Maple-Glazed Salmon Fillets

Truly a Canadian dish! Maple syrup gives the salmon a unique, sweet flavor.

Maple-Soy Marinade:

⅓ cup	unsweetened apple juice	75 mL
⅓ cup	pure maple syrup	75 mL
2 tbsp.	soy sauce	30 mL
1 tbsp.	lemon juice	15 mL
2 tbsp.	finely chopped onion	30 mL
2	garlic cloves, minced	2
2 lbs.	salmon fillets	1 kg

Marinade: In a small bowl, combine apple juice, maple syrup, soy sauce, lemon juice, onion and garlic. Remove ½ cup (125 mL) of sauce for basting; cover and refrigerate. Pour remaining marinade into a large resealable plastic bag.

Add salmon to marinade; reseal bag and turn to coat salmon. Place in refrigerator for 1-3 hours. Preheat barbecue or preheat oven for broiling. Drain and discard marinade. Broil salmon 4" (10 cm) from heat for 5 minutes. Baste with reserved marinade. Broil 10 minutes longer, or until fish flakes easily with a fork, basting frequently. Serve immediately.

Serves 4

Pictured on the front cover.

Salmon is low in calories and saturated fats, yet high in protein and a unique type of health-promoting fat, the omega-3 essential fatty acids. These acids are essential for human health but because they cannot be made by the body, they must be obtained from foods. As well as an excellent source of ometa-3s and selenium, salmon is a good source of protein, niacin, vitamin B_{12}, phosphorous, magnesium and vitamin B_6.

Baked Salmon with Rice Dressing

An elegant and delicious presentation!

1 tbsp.	olive oil	15 mL
1½ cups	sliced mushrooms	375 mL
½ cup	chopped celery	125 mL
½ cup	shredded carrot	125 mL
¼ cup	chopped green onion	60 mL
¼ cup	chopped fresh parsley	60 mL
¾ cup	long-grain rice	175 mL
2½ cups	chicken stock	625 mL
¼ tsp.	pepper	1 mL
4-6 lbs.	fresh salmon, washed and patted dry	1.8-2.5 kg
¼ cup	lemon juice	60 mL

Preheat oven to 350°F (180°C). In a large frying pan, heat oil over medium heat, cook mushrooms, celery, carrot, green onion and parsley until tender. Add rice, chicken stock and pepper. Cook, covered, over low heat for 20 minutes, or until rice is tender and liquid is absorbed. Remove from heat.

Rinse salmon and pat dry. If salmon is whole, stuff loosely and place in a 10 x 15" (25 x 38 cm) baking dish. If salmon is in steaks or fillets, place salmon over stuffing in a 12" (30 cm) ovenproof frying pan or baking dish. Sprinkle the salmon with lemon juice. Bake, covered, for 1-1½ hours, or until fish flakes easily. Serve with lemon wedges.

Serves 8-12 .

Baked Salmon with Tarragon

This is Jo's recipe. She cooks salmon at least once a week and uses this recipe often – it always turns out moist, has great flavor and looks picture perfect.

1½ lbs.	fresh salmon fillets	750 g
2 tbsp.	light mayonnaise	30 mL
1	large onion, sliced	1
2 tbsp.	brown sugar	30 mL
2-3 tbsp.	lemon juice	30-45 mL
3 tbsp.	fresh tarragon or 2 tsp. (10 mL) dried	45 mL

Preheat oven to 350°F (180°C). Rinse fillets, pat dry and place on a baking sheet. Brush or spread mayonnaise evenly over fillets. Separate sliced onions into rings and arrange over fillets. Spoon brown sugar evenly over top. Sprinkle lemon juice over fillets; top with a sprinkling of tarragon. Bake for 15-20 minutes, or until easily flaked with a fork. (Do not over bake). Remove and discard onion. Transfer salmon to a serving plate.

Serves 4-6

Breaded Baked Perch

Delicious with any fish fillets; try your favorites.

½ cup	dry whole-wheat bread crumbs	125 mL
2 tbsp.	grated Parmesan cheese	30 mL
1 tbsp.	paprika	15 mL
1 tsp.	dried basil	5 mL
2 tbsp.	butter OR margarine, melted	30 mL
2 lbs.	perch fillets	1 kg

Preheat oven to 500°F (260°C). In a shallow bowl or pie plate, combine bread crumbs, Parmesan cheese, paprika and basil. Brush fish fillets with butter, then dip into the crumb mixture to coat. Place on a lightly buttered baking sheet. Bake, uncovered, for 10-15 minutes, or until fish flakes easily with a fork.

Serves 4-6

Baked Sole Topped with Crab and Parmesan

An elegant presentation for a special occasion.

6 oz.	can crabmeat, drained, flaked and cartilage removed	180 g
½ cup	grated Parmesan cheese	125 mL
½ cup	low-fat mayonnaise	125 mL
1 tsp.	lemon juice	5 mL
1 lb.	sole fillets	500 g
½ tsp.	paprika	2 mL
⅓ cup	slivered almonds, toasted	75 mL

Preheat oven to 350°F (180°C). In a small bowl, combine crab, Parmesan cheese, mayonnaise and lemon juice. Stir well and set aside. Place sole fillets on a lightly buttered baking sheet. Bake, uncovered, for 15-20 minutes, or until fish flakes easily with a fork. Remove fish from oven; drain cooking juices from baking dish. Spoon crab mixture evenly over the fillets. Broil 5" (13 cm) from the heat for 5 minutes, or until crab topping is lightly browned. Remove from oven; sprinkle with paprika and toasted almonds. Serve immediately.

Serves 4

Fish contain high-quality protein, are low in saturated fat and are a good source of vitamins and essential minerals. Studies recommend at least two servings of fish per week for cardio-protective effects. Each type of fish provides different health benefits. Fatty fish are an excellent source of omega-3 fatty acids which help reduce the risks of heart disease and certain cancers, protect circulation, and play an important role in brain development.

Some examples of FATTY (oily) FISH are: trout, salmon, mackerel, herring, sardines, tuna (fresh only), anchovies, Jackfish, orange roughy. LEAN FISH include: cod, haddock, plaice, sole, halibut, catfish, flounder, monkfish, pollack, red snapper, sea bass, canned tuna.

Baked Sole With Pineapple Sauce

Peppery pineapple sauce creates a superb contrast to this baked sole.

Peppery Pineapple Sauce:

19 oz.	can unsweetened pineapple chunks, drained, juice reserved	540 mL
⅓ cup	chicken stock	75 mL
1 tbsp.	sugar	15 mL
1 tbsp.	cider vinegar	15 mL
1½ tsp.	cornstarch	7 mL
¼ tsp.	ground ginger	1 mL
6-8 drops	hot pepper sauce	6-8 drops
¼ cup	sliced green onions	60 mL
½ cup	sliced water chestnuts	125 mL
4	sole fillets (approximately ½"/1.3 cm thick)	4
1 tbsp.	butter OR margarine	15 mL
½ cup	whole-wheat bread crumbs	125 mL
¼ tsp.	paprika	1 mL

Preheat oven to 400°F (200°C).

Sauce: Drain pineapple; reserve juice. From reserved juice measure ⅓ cup (75 mL) liquid. In a small saucepan, whisk together reserved juice, chicken stock, sugar, vinegar, cornstarch, ginger and hot pepper sauce. Place over medium heat; cook, stirring constantly, until sauce boils and thickens, about 4-5 minutes. Remove from heat, stir in green onions, water chestnuts and pineapple; keep warm.

Arrange fish fillets in a lightly buttered 9 x 13" (23 x 33 cm) baking pan; drizzle with melted butter, then sprinkle with bread crumbs and paprika. Bake for 8-15 minutes, or until fish is easily flaked with a fork. Serve immediately with pineapple sauce.

Serves 4

Broccoli and Chicken Stir-Fry

Orange juice enhances the flavor of the chicken and provides a unique sauce.

1 lb.	boneless, skinless chicken breast, cut into 1" (2.5 cm) pieces	500 g

Orange Sauce:

1 cup	unsweetened orange juice	250 mL
1 tbsp.	cornstarch	15 mL
1 tbsp.	dry white wine OR water	15 mL
1 tbsp.	soy sauce	15 mL
½ tsp.	ground ginger	2 mL
1 tbsp.	olive oil	15 mL
4 cups	broccoli florets	1 L
1 cup	sliced mushrooms	250 mL
½ cup	EACH sliced onion and celery, diagonally sliced	125 mL
2 tbsp.	toasted sliced almonds	30 mL

Rinse chicken, pat dry and cut into 1" (2.5 cm) pieces; set aside.

Sauce: In a small bowl, combine orange juice, cornstarch, white wine, soy sauce and ginger. Stir well to combine; set aside.

In a wok or large frying pan, heat oil over medium heat; add broccoli, mushrooms, onion and celery; stir-fry for 2-3 minutes. With a slotted spoon, remove vegetables to a platter. Add chicken pieces; stir-fry 4-5 minutes, or until tender and no longer pink. Stir sauce mixture; add to frying pan. Cook, stirring constantly, for 2-3 minutes, or until sauce is bubbling and slightly thickened. Return vegetables to frying pan; stir all ingredients together to coat with sauce. Sprinkle with almonds.

Serves 4

Mediterranean Herbed Chicken

A taste of the Mediterranean in this time-honored dish – delicious with either fettuccini or rice.

1 tbsp.	olive oil	15 mL
½ cup	chopped onion	125 mL
1½ lbs.	boneless, skinless, chicken breasts, cut into 1" (2.5 cm) pieces	750 g
1	small green pepper, cut into strips	1
1	small red pepper, cut into strips	1
2	garlic cloves, minced	2
3	small zucchini, sliced	3
4	large tomatoes, chopped	4
½ tsp.	dried oregano	2 mL
1 tsp.	dried basil	5 mL
½ cup	sliced kalamata olives	125 mL
½ cup	shredded fresh Parmesan cheese	125 mL

Heat oil in a large frying pan over medium-high heat until hot. Add onion; cook for 2-3 minutes or until tender, stirring often. Add chicken, peppers and garlic; mixing well. Cook for 5-6 minutes, or until chicken is browned and no longer pink in center, stirring occasionally. Add zucchini, tomatoes, oregano, basil and olives; cook for 5-6 minutes, or until zucchini is tender, stirring occasionally. Serve over fettuccine or rice. Sprinkle with Parmesan cheese.

Serves 6

Pictured opposite.

Tomatoes, especially cooked or processed, are a good source of vitamin C and potassium. They are high in phytochemicals, including lycopene, an antioxidant nutrient, which helps provide disease prevention benefits – heart disease prevention plus prostate and digestive tract cancer prevention. Ounce for ounce, processed tomato products such as sauce, paste or juice contain 2 to 10 times as much available lycopene as fresh tomatoes.

Main Course – Chicken

Mediterranean Herbed Chicken, page 120
Lemon Broccoli Sauté, page 91
Rice and Noodle Pilaf, page 98

Baked Chicken and Cranberries

Honey, lemon and cranberries make a beautiful sauce for this special chicken dish.

Honey-Roasted Cranberries:

3½ cups	fresh cranberries or frozen, thawed	825 mL
⅓ cup	sugar	75 mL
2 tbsp.	cornstarch	30 mL
½ cup	liquid honey	125 mL
1 tbsp.	lemon juice	15 mL
8	boneless, skinless chicken breasts	8
1 tbsp.	olive oil	15 mL
¼ cup	orange juice	60 mL
1 tbsp.	grated orange zest	15 mL
¼ tsp.	EACH salt and pepper	1 mL

Preheat oven to 375°F (190°C).

Sauce: Place cranberries in a lightly buttered 9 x 13" (23 x 33 cm) baking dish. In a small bowl, stir together sugar and cornstarch; sprinkle over cranberries. Mix together honey and lemon juice and drizzle over cranberries. Bake for 15-20 minutes, stirring once through the cooking process. Remove from oven and set aside.

Pat chicken breasts dry. In a large frying pan, heat oil over medium-high heat, brown chicken for about 5-8 minutes, turning once. Place chicken breasts on top of cranberry mixture. Drizzle with orange juice and sprinkle with orange zest, salt and pepper. Bake for 30-45 minutes, or until chicken is no longer pink inside. Transfer chicken to a serving platter. Stir sauce well and spoon over chicken. Serve immediately.

Serves 8

Crispy Potato Chicken

This recipe takes a little extra effort to prepare, but is well worth it. The coating ensures a moist, flavorful chicken breast.

1	large potato, peeled, shredded	1
2	large whole skinless chicken breasts, cut in half (4 halves)	2
3 tbsp.	Dijon mustard	45 mL
2	garlic cloves, minced	2
1½ tsp.	olive oil	7 mL
⅛ tsp.	pepper	0.5 mL
1 tbsp.	snipped fresh parsley	15 mL

Preheat oven to 425°F (220°C). In a food processor fitted with a medium shredding disk or with a grater, coarsely shred the potato. Transfer shredded potato to a bowl of ice water; allow to stand for 5 minutes. Rinse chicken under cold water and thoroughly pat dry. In a small bowl, stir together mustard and garlic; mix well. Brush or spread the mustard mixture evenly on the meaty side of the chicken breast halves. Place the chicken bone side down on a foil-lined 10 x 15" (25 x 38 cm) baking sheet. Drain shredded potato; thoroughly pat dry with paper towels. In a small bowl, combine shredded potato and olive oil; toss to mix well. Top each piece of chicken with about ⅓ cup (75 mL) of potato mixture in an even layer, forming a "skin". Sprinkle lightly with pepper. Cook for 35-45 minutes, or until chicken is no longer pink and potato shreds are golden. If potatoes are not browning, place pan under broiler; broil for 3-5 minutes or until golden, watching closely. Sprinkle with fresh parsley. Serve immediately.

Serves 4

Slow-Cooker Chicken in Pineapple Sauce

A simple classic that never goes out of style.

1½ lbs.	boneless, skinless chicken breast, cut into ½" (1.3 cm) strips	750 g
2 tbsp.	soy sauce	30 mL
2	medium carrots, sliced	2
½ cup	chopped celery	125 mL
10 oz.	can water chestnuts, drained, sliced	284 g
14 oz.	can unsweetened pineapple chunks in juice, drained, reserving juice	398 mL
½ cup	pineapple juice OR apple juice	125 mL
1 tbsp.	cornstarch	15 mL
1½ cups	snow peas	375 mL
3	green onions, cut into 1" (2.5 cm) pieces	3

In a 4-quart (4 L) slow cooker, combine chicken and soy sauce; mix to coat evenly. Add carrots, celery, water chestnuts and reserved pineapple juice. Stir to combine. Cover, cook on low setting for 4-5 hours. About 30 minutes before serving, in a small bowl, combine pineapple juice or apple juice and cornstarch; stir until well blended. Stir into chicken mixture. Add snow peas, onions and pineapple chunks; stir gently to mix. Increase heat setting to high; cover and cook an additional 20-25 minutes, or until snow peas are crisp-tender. Serve over rice.

Serves 6

Green peas provide nutrients that help support the energy-producing cells and systems of the body. Instrumental to the body's blood clotting ability, they are important for maintaining bone health; aid cardiovascular function; help to prevent virtually all types of cancer. Peas are a very good source of vitamin K, manganese, vitamin C, dietary fiber, thiamin and folate.

Cranberry-Glazed Stir-Fried Turkey

This beautiful dish is full of tart, sweet flavor.

1 tbsp.	olive oil	15 mL
2	garlic cloves, minced	2
2 cups	julienne-cut carrots	500 mL
½ cup	diagonally sliced celery	125 ml
2 cups	boneless, skinless turkey breast, cut into strips	500 mL
2 cups	julienne-cut zucchini	500 mL
2 cups	broccoli florets	500 mL
8 oz.	can jellied cranberry sauce	250 mL
⅓ cup	unsweetened apple juice	75 mL
3 tbsp.	soy sauce	45 mL
¼ cup	cider vinegar	60 mL
1 tsp.	cornstarch	5 mL
¼ cup	cold water	60 mL

In a large frying pan or wok, heat oil over medium-high and stir-fry garlic for 30 seconds. Add carrots and celery; stir-fry for 2 minutes. Add turkey, zucchini and broccoli; stir-fry for 3 minutes. In a small bowl, combine cranberry sauce, apple juice, soy sauce and vinegar until smooth; gradually stir into frying pan. Bring to a boil. In a small bowl, combine cornstarch and water until smooth; gradually stir into skillet. Bring to a boil; cook and stir for 1-2 minutes, or until thickened and bubbly and turkey juices run clear. Serve immediately.

Serves 4

Cranberries are loaded with phytochemicals that are effective in preventing prostate, colon, breast, leukemia, head and neck cancers. For hundreds of years, they have been prized for their ability to reduce the risk of urinary tract infections. (1 cup/250 mL of cranberry juice per day has been suggested as the best amount for significant bladder infection protection, but medical advice is advised if an infection is already present.) Cranberry juice helps prevent kidney stone formation, supports gastrointestinal and oral health (reducing tooth decay), lowers LDL (bad) cholesterol and provides cardiovascular benefits.

Apple and Cinnamon Pork Stir-Fry

Honey and cinnamon, lime and apple juices create a mouthwatering pork marinade. This is a lovely autumn or winter dish.

Apple Cinnamon Marinade:

¼ cup	unsweetened apple juice	60 mL
¼ cup	chicken stock	60 mL
3 tbsp.	soy sauce	45 mL
2 tbsp.	liquid honey	30 mL
½ tsp.	ground cinnamon	2 mL
1 tbsp.	lime juice	15 mL
1 tsp.	cornstarch	5 mL
1 lb.	pork tenderloin or boneless chops, cut into 1" (2.5 cm) slices	500 g
1 tbsp.	olive oil	15 mL
1	sliced red onion	1
1	small zucchini, sliced	1
1 cup	sliced cabbage	250 mL
2	apples, peeled, cored and cubed	2

Marinade: In a medium bowl, combine apple juice, chicken stock, soy sauce, honey, cinnamon, lime juice and cornstarch.

Add pork slices to the marinade and set aside. In a large frying pan or wok, heat oil over medium-high heat; add onion and stir-fry for 1 minute. Using a slotted spoon, remove pork from bowl, saving marinade. Add pork slices to wok and stir-fry 2-3 minutes, or until browned. Remove pork from pan; set aside. Add zucchini, cabbage and apple; stir-fry 1 minute. Add saved marinade to pan and bring to a boil. Cook, stirring constantly, for 3-4 minutes. Return browned pork slices to pan and cook until heated through. Serve immediately with rice or noodles.

Serves 4

Fruited Pork Tenderloin

An impressive dish that is quick to fix – tender, succulent pork with a tangy apricot sauce.

1 lb.	pork tenderloin OR boneless chops	500 g
1 tbsp.	olive oil	15 mL
12 oz.	can apricot nectar	341 mL
½ cup	quartered dried apricots	125 mL
½ cup	sliced green onions	125 mL
2 tbsp.	chicken stock	30 mL
¼ tsp.	ground ginger	1 mL
1 tbsp.	cornstarch	15 mL
2 tbsp.	cold water	30 mL

Cut pork crosswise into 1" (2.5 cm) thick slices. In a large frying pan or wok, heat oil over medium-high heat. Add pork and stir-fry for 3-5 minutes, or until no pink shows through. Add nectar, apricots, onions, chicken stock and ginger. Bring to a boil; reduce heat, cover and simmer 5 minutes. Remove pork from skillet; keep warm. In a small bowl, combine cornstarch and cold water; stir into sauce in skillet. Cook, stirring constantly, until thickened and bubbly, about 3 minutes. Return cooked pork to frying pan; heat through. Serve immediately over rice or pasta.

Serves 4

Apricots contain nutrients that can help protect the heart and eyes. They are rich in vitamin A, which promotes good vision, and their high lycopene and beta-carotene content makes them important heart health foods. Dried apricots are also rich in iron and calcium and a good source of fiber.

Pork Chops in Herbed Mustard Sauce

Tender pork chops in a rich, creamy mustard sauce with just a hint of garlic and tarragon.

1 tsp.	olive oil	5 mL
4	boneless pork loin chops, trimmed of all fat	4

Herbed Mustard Sauce:

¼ cup	dry white wine	60 mL
2	garlic cloves, minced	2
¾ cup	chicken stock	175 mL
2 tsp.	cornstarch	10 mL
1 tbsp.	cold water	15 mL
½ cup	light sour cream	125 mL
1 tbsp.	Dijon mustard	15 mL
1 tbsp.	chopped fresh tarragon OR chopped fresh chives	15 mL

Heat oil in a large frying pan over medium-high heat. Add pork chops and fry until brown, about 3-5 minutes on each side. Transfer to a plate; set aside and keep warm.

Sauce: Add wine to frying pan with garlic and let it bubble briefly over medium-high heat. Pour in stock and boil for 2 minutes. In a small bowl, whisk together cornstarch and cold water; add sour cream and mix until smooth. Add to the cooking liquid, stirring well. Reduce heat and simmer, stirring constantly, until thick and smooth, about 2 minutes. Stir in mustard and tarragon.

Return pork chops to the sauce in the frying pan. Reduce heat to low, cover pan and simmer until the chops are completely cooked through, 5-8 minutes. Serve immediately.

Serves 4

Lemon-Baked Pork Chops

Lemon and rosemary are classic flavorings with pork. These baked chops are tender, tasty and terrific.

½ cup	dry whole-wheat bread crumbs	125 mL
¼ cup	grated Parmesan cheese	60 mL
¼ tsp.	salt	1 mL
½ tsp.	crushed dried rosemary	2 mL
½ tsp.	grated lemon zest OR lemon pepper seasoning	2 mL
1	egg, lightly beaten	1
¼ cup	dry white wine OR apple juice	60 mL
1 tbsp.	lemon juice	15 mL
1 tsp.	olive oil	5 mL
6	pork chops, trimmed of all fat	6

Preheat oven to 350°F (180°C). In a shallow container, or pie plate, combine bread crumbs, Parmesan cheese, salt, rosemary and lemon zest; stir well to combine and set aside. In a medium bowl, whisk egg with wine, lemon juice and oil. Dip chops into egg mixture; dredge in bread crumb mixture and place on a broiler pan or a rack in a roasting pan. Bake for 40-45 minutes, or until tender. Serve garnished with lemon slices.

Serves 6

Slow Cooker Sauerkraut and Ribs

Sauerkraut and ribs are a favorite in our family. With this easy method, place everything in the slow cooker before work and supper is ready as soon as you get home.

3 lbs.	pork loin ribs	1.5 kg
1	medium cooking apple, sliced	1
1	small onion, sliced	1
16 oz.	can sauerkraut, drained, rinsed	454 g
2 tbsp.	brown sugar	30 mL
1 tsp.	caraway seed (optional)	5 mL
¼ cup	dry white wine OR apple juice	60 mL

Place pork ribs, apple and onion in a 4-5-quart (4-5 L) slow cooker. Top with sauerkraut, brown sugar and caraway seeds; mix lightly. Pour wine or apple juice over. Cover and cook on low setting for 8-10 hours.

Serves 6

Apples, with peels, are nutritional powerhouses. They contain soluble and insoluble fiber which lowers LDL (bad) cholesterol, reducing the risk of hardening of the arteries, heart attack and stroke. They also promote bowel regularity, reducing cancer risk. The flavenoids in apples significantly reduce the risk of heart disease. The fructose and fiber in apples help keep blood sugar levels stable. Apples help to prevent kidney stones, protect against breast cancer and have beneficial effects against asthma and diabetes. A whole apple a day (with peel) will help keep the doctor away!

Tomato, Beef and Pasta

Prepare this flavorful pasta sauce in less time than it takes to cook the pasta.

3 cups	uncooked corkscrew pasta, cooked and drained	750 mL
1 lb.	extra-lean ground beef	500 g
2	garlic cloves, minced	2
7	green onions, diagonally sliced into 2" (5 cm) pieces	7
2 tbsp.	Worcestershire sauce	30 mL
3	stalks celery, diagonally sliced into 1" (2.5 cm) pieces	3
1 cup	sliced mushrooms	250 mL
1 cup	snow peas	250 mL
8 oz.	can tomato sauce	213 mL
3	tomatoes, cut into wedges	3
1 cup	low-fat shredded Cheddar cheese, divided	250 mL
1	green OR red pepper, cut into thin slices	1

Cook pasta as directed on package; rinse, drain and set aside. In a large frying pan over medium-high heat, cook beef, garlic, onions and Worcestershire sauce, until meat is browned and no pink is showing. Add celery and mushrooms; stir-fry for 2 minutes. Add snow peas and tomato sauce; cook for 4-5 minutes, stirring constantly. Add cooked pasta, tomatoes and ¾ cup (175 mL) of the cheese. Stir gently; cook for 1 minute. Add peppers; sprinkle with remaining cheese. Reduce heat to low; cook until heated through. Serve immediately.

Serves 4-6

Extra-Lean Chili

Chili is a real comfort food and also a very healthy choice – beans and tomatoes add fiber and many health benefits; spicy foods boost metabolism. This is an all-around winner.

1½ lbs.	extra-lean ground beef	750 g
1	small green OR red pepper, chopped	1
2	garlic cloves, minced	2
1	onion, chopped	1
1 cup	beef stock	250 mL
15 oz.	can red kidney beans, drained	425 mL
28 oz.	can tomatoes with juice	796 mL
2-3 tsp.	chili powder	10-15 mL
½ tsp.	dried oregano	2 mL
½ tsp.	ground cumin	2 mL
½ tsp.	ground coriander	2 mL
½ tsp.	salt	2 mL
¼ tsp.	pepper	1 mL

In a large frying pan over medium-high heat, cook beef, peppers, garlic and onion, stirring constantly, until meat is browned and no pink is showing. Drain off all fat (see note below). Add beef stock to skillet; reduce heat to medium and cook for 5-10 minutes. Add beans, tomatoes with juice, chili powder, oregano, cumin, coriander, salt and pepper; stir to combine. Bring chili to a boil; reduce heat and simmer, uncovered, for 20-25 minutes, stirring occasionally. Serve immediately.

Serves 4-6

Variation: For the kidney beans, substitute or add a can of mixed beans, black beans or chickpeas. For **Turkey Chili**, substitute ground turkey for the ground beef. For a **Fiery Chili**, double the amount of chili powder and cumin and add hot pepper sauce to taste.

For best fat removal, drain ground beef in a colander, then rinse with very hot water. The recipe flavor will not be affected.

Beef Porcupines in Tomato Sauce

These simple, moist and flavorful meatballs topped with a tomato sauce are a true favorite with our family. An easy-to-prepare recipe.

1 lb.	extra-lean ground beef	250 mL
½ cup	short-grain rice	125 mL
¼ cup	chopped onion	60 mL
½ tsp.	salt	2 mL
¼ tsp.	pepper	1 mL
2 cups	tomato juice OR vegetable juice cocktail	500 mL

Preheat oven to 350°F (180°C). In a large bowl, combine beef, rice, onions, salt and pepper; mix well. Form into 1½" (4 cm) balls (a small ice-cream scoop is a big help). Place balls in a 10" (25 cm) ovenproof frying pan or baking dish. Pour tomato juice over the meatballs. Bake, covered, for 1 hour; uncover and bake 30 minutes more.

Serves 4

Meatballs in Pineapple Sauce

Onion-flavored meatballs in a tangy sweet and sour sauce. The pineapple chunks give it a Hawaiian touch and great flavor.

Meatballs:

1½ lbs.	extra-lean ground beef	750 g
⅓ cup	finely chopped onion	75 mL
½ tsp.	salt	2 mL
½ tsp.	pepper	2 mL
1-2 tbsp.	milk	15-30 mL

Pineapple Sauce:

14 oz.	can unsweetened pineapple chunks, drained, reserving juice	398 mL
2 tbsp.	cornstarch	30 mL
½ cup	brown sugar	125 mL
⅛ cup	white vinegar	30 mL
½ cup	ketchup	125 mL
1 tbsp.	soy sauce	15 mL

Meatballs: Preheat oven to 375°F (190°C). In a large bowl, combine all meatball ingredients and mix well. Form mixture into meatballs (a small ice-cream scoop is a big help) and place on a broiler pan. Bake for 25-30 minutes, or until no pink is showing. Remove from oven and set aside.

Sauce: Drain pineapple chunks, reserving juice; set aside. In a medium-sized saucepan, combine cornstarch, brown sugar, vinegar, ketchup, reserved pineapple juice and soy sauce. Place over medium heat and bring to a boil, stirring constantly. Add pineapple chunks; continue to cook for 2 minutes.

Preheat oven to 300°F (150°C). Transfer meatballs to a Dutch oven or small roasting pan. Pour sauce over meatballs; cover and bake for 45-60 minutes.

Serves 6-8

Oriental-Style Beef and Vegetables

For quick and easy meal preparation, serve with rice or noodles.

1 tbsp.	olive oil	15 mL
3 cups	shredded green cabbage	750 mL
1 lb.	beef sirloin steak, cut into strips	500 g
2	large onions, sliced and separated into rings	2
3	stalks celery, sliced	3
1 lb.	bean sprouts, washed and drained	500 g
10 oz.	can bamboo shoots, drained	284 mL
10 oz.	can sliced water chestnuts, drained	284 mL
2 tbsp.	liquid honey	30 mL
1 tsp.	cornstarch	5 mL
½ cup	beef stock	125 mL
3 tbsp.	soy sauce	45 mL

In a large frying pan or wok, heat oil over medium-high heat and stir-fry cabbage until it begins to soften. Add beef; cook and stir for 3 minutes. Add onions, celery and bean sprouts; stir-fry for 2-3 minutes, or until vegetables are tender-crisp. Add bamboo shoots and water chestnuts. In a small bowl, combine honey, cornstarch, beef stock and soy sauce until smooth; stir into beef mixture. Bring to a boil; cook and stir for 2 minutes, or until thickened and vegetables are tender. Serve immediately.

Serves 6-8

Beef Stroganoff Stir-Fry

Zesty horseradish spices up this classic dish.

2 tbsp.	olive oil, divided	30 mL
3 cups	button-sized mushrooms	750 mL
1	red pepper, seeded and cut into strips	1
1½ cups	broccoli, cut into small florets	375 mL
⅔ cup	beef stock	150 mL
2 tsp.	Worcestershire sauce	10 mL
3	garlic cloves, minced	3
1	onion, sliced	1
1 lb.	beef steak or tenderloin, cut into thin strips	500 g
3 tbsp.	prepared horseradish	45 mL
⅔ cup	light sour cream	150 mL

Heat half of the oil in a large frying pan over medium heat. Add mushrooms and sauté about 2 minutes, or until they begin to soften. Stir in red pepper and broccoli and continue to cook, stirring frequently, for 3-4 minutes. Pour in beef stock and Worcestershire sauce; bring to a boil. Reduce heat, cover and allow to simmer until broccoli is just tender, about 4-5 minutes. Transfer to a bowl and set aside. In the same frying pan, add remaining oil and heat over medium-high heat. Add garlic and onion and sauté until soft, about 3 minutes. Add beef strips and cook until beef has changed color and no pink is showing. Reduce heat to medium-low; stir in horseradish and sour cream. Add vegetables with their cooking liquid and continue to cook until vegetables are heated through, about 3-4 minutes. Serve immediately.

Serves 4

Old-Fashioned Beef Stew

A true comfort food – wonderful with homemade bread.

1½ lbs.	beef stew meat or round steak cut into 1" (2.5 cm) cubes	750 g
1	large onion, cut into 1" (2.5 cm) pieces	1
1 cup	celery, cut into 1" (2.5 cm) pieces	250 mL
3 cups	vegetable juice cocktail	750 mL
2 cups	beef stock	500 mL
2 tsp.	Worcestershire sauce	10 mL
¼ cup	pearl barley	60 mL
2	large carrots, cut into 1" (2.5 cm) slices	2
4	medium potatoes, cut into 1" (2.5 cm) cubes	4
½	small turnip, cut into 1" (2.5 cm) cubes	½
¾ cup	frozen peas	175 mL

In a large frying pan, over medium-high heat, brown beef on all sides. Cook 2-3 minutes each side, or until well browned. Transfer meat to a large saucepan or Dutch oven; add onion, celery, vegetable juice, beef stock and Worcestershire sauce. Cover and place over low heat. Allow stew to simmer for 2 hours, checking to ensure all meat and vegetables are totally covered in liquid. Add additional vegetable juice or beef stock if necessary. Add pearl barley, carrots, potatoes and turnip; stir to combine and continue to simmer stew over low heat for additional 45-60 minutes, or until vegetables are tender. Add frozen peas 15-20 minutes before serving.

Serves 6-8

Savory Pot Roast and Vegetables

A great "taste-of-home" kind of meal. Because of the long cooking time, this is wonderful to make on a cold day when you want to stay indoors.

1 tbsp.	olive oil	15 mL
3-5 lb.	cross rib OR chuck beef roast	1.5-2.2 kg
¼ cup	water	60 mL
5	medium carrots, pared, halved	5
5	medium potatoes, pared, halved	5
2	medium onions, peeled, quartered	2
1	small head of cabbage, cored, quartered	1
½ tsp.	salt	2 mL
¼ tsp.	pepper	1 mL

Heat oil in a Dutch oven or large roasting pan over medium-high heat. Brown roast on all sides, turning with tongs. Add water, cover and reduce heat to low. Allow roast to cook on low for 1½-2 hours. Turn roast, add all vegetables; sprinkle with salt and pepper. Continue to simmer, covered, on low heat for 1-1½ hours, or until vegetables are tender.

Serves 6-10

Mediterranean-Style Swiss Steak

Slow baking in a savory wine broth makes this steak very tender and flavorful.

1 tbsp.	olive oil	15 mL
1½-2 lb.	boneless beef round steak, trimmed of fat	750 g-1 kg
1	medium onion, coarsely chopped	1
½ cup	coarsely chopped celery	125 mL
1	large carrot, thinly sliced	1
1	coarsely chopped green OR red pepper	1
2	garlic cloves, minced	2
28 oz.	can tomatoes with juice	796 mL
8 oz.	can tomato sauce	250 mL
½ cup	dry red wine	125 mL
1 tbsp.	Worcestershire sauce	15 mL
1½ tsp.	Italian seasoning	7 mL
¼ tsp.	salt	1 mL
⅛ tsp.	pepper	0.5 mL

Preheat oven to 325°F (160°C). Heat oil in a Dutch oven over medium-high heat; brown steak on both sides. Cook for 2-3 minutes on each side, or until well browned; turning only once. Transfer steak to a plate; set aside. To Dutch oven, add onion, celery, carrots, peppers and garlic; sauté for 3-5 minutes, or just until vegetables are tender. Stir in tomatoes with juice, tomato sauce, wine, Worcestershire sauce and seasonings. Cut the browned steak into 4 pieces; return to Dutch oven. Cover and bake for 1½-2 hours, or until meat is tender; turn steak once through cooking period. Serve with spaghetti or rice.

Serves 4

Desserts

Fresh Fruit
Frozen Fruit Desserts
Cheesecakes
Puddings
Baked Fruits

Fruits Ahoy

These are especially showy – cantaloupe boats filled with cantaloupe balls and berries. A light and refreshing ending to a meal.

Balsamic Orange Glaze:

¼ cup	balsamic vinegar	60 mL
1 tsp.	grated orange zest	5 mL
2 tbsp.	fresh orange juice	30 mL
2 tsp.	brown sugar	10 mL
1	large cantaloupe	1
2 cups	strawberries, hulled and quartered	500 mL
1 cup	EACH blueberries and raspberries	250 mL
	Grand Marnier (optional)	

Glaze: In a small saucepan, combine vinegar, orange zest, orange juice and brown sugar. Cook over medium-high heat until syrupy, about 4-5 minutes. Remove from heat and set aside.

To prepare cantaloupe, cut lengthwise in half and remove all seeds. Then cut each melon half in half crosswise to form triangular boats. Make melon balls by scooping out cantaloupe meat with a melon baller, leaving a thin layer of flesh on the rind. Place cantaloupe balls in a large bowl; add strawberries, blueberries and raspberries. Mix gently to combine. Drizzle fruit with Balsamic Orange glaze; toss gently to coat evenly. Spoon fruit into cantaloupe boats, drizzle with Grand Marnier and serve immediately.

Serves 4

Pictured on page 17.

Cantaloupe is an excellent source of beta-carotene and vitamin A, important vision and emphysema protection nutrients. It is also an excellent source of vitamin C, which is critical for good immune function. 1 cup (250 mL) of cantaloupe a day provides 100 percent of the daily value for both vitamins A and C. Cantaloupe is a very good source of potassium and a good source of B complex vitamins and fiber.

Fruit Delight

Elegant and refreshing – fresh fruit served with an orange dressing laced with brandy.

4	oranges, peeled and sectioned	4
2	bananas, peeled and sliced	2
1½ cups	pineapple chunks	375 mL
1 cup	green grapes	250 mL

Orange Brandy Sauce:

½ tsp.	grated orange zest	2 mL
¼ cup	unsweetened orange juice	60 mL
2 tbsp.	icing (confectioner's) sugar	30 mL
1 tbsp.	brandy (optional)	15 mL
2 tbsp.	toasted coconut	30 mL

Arrange orange sections in the bottom of a large glass serving bowl. Dip banana slices in a little orange juice, turning to coat; layer bananas over the orange sections. Add pineapple chunks in a layer over the bananas. Sprinkle green grapes on top.

Sauce: In a small bowl, stir together orange zest, orange juice, icing (confectioner's) sugar and brandy. Spoon sauce over fruit. Cover and refrigerate for 1-2 hours. Sprinkle with toasted coconut just before serving.

Serves 6-8

Citrus zest nutrients can help reduce the incidence of skin cancer. D-limonene, found in orange, lemon and grapefruit peel, has been shown to help protect against a variety of cancers. Compounds in orange and tangerine zest also lower LDL (bad) cholesterol. 1 tbsp. (15 mL) of zest per week, approximately the zest of 1 orange or lemon, is the amount recommended by University of Arizona researchers. Add citrus zest to muffins, salads, fish, meats and desserts for a delicious, tangy flavor.

Fruit Quartet with Orange Cream Cheese Sauce

Layer fruit in a glass bowl for a "showy" presentation. Topped with a light, creamy orange sauce, this dessert is the perfect ending to a steak barbecue.

Orange Cream Cheese Sauce:

8 oz.	light cream cheese, softened	250 g
2 tbsp.	unsweetened orange juice	30 mL
1 tsp.	grated orange zest	5 mL
½ cup	whipped cream, page 146	125 mL
2 cups	sliced fresh peaches	500 mL
2 cups	fresh blueberries	500 mL
2 cups	sliced fresh strawberries	500 mL
2 cups	whole green grapes	500 mL
½ cup	chopped walnuts OR pecans, toasted	125 mL

Sauce: In a small bowl, with an electric mixer, beat cream cheese, orange juice and orange zest until smooth and well blended. Fold in whipped cream and combine well; refrigerate until ready to serve.

Layer fruit in a 1½-quart (1.5 L) glass serving bowl. Top with cream cheese sauce; sprinkle with nuts. Serve immediately.

Serves 8-10

 Cream is rich in vitamin A and has half the calories of vegetable oils, butter and margarine. Dairy foods are high in calcium, riboflavin, magnesium, phosphorus, vitamin B_{12} and protein. If you want a lower-fat substitute, see the recipe on page 146, or you can also whip evaporated milk – place evaporated milk in freezer until partially frozen; pour into a chilled bowl; add vanilla and beat on high until stiff. Avoid trans-fat-laden whipped toppings which contain hydrogenated palm and coconut oils.

Peaches with a Berry Trio

Make this when luscious, juicy peaches are in season. Peaches and fresh berries are topped with a creamy, candied ginger sauce – Superb!!

Ginger Yogurt Sauce:

½ cup	low-fat plain yogurt	125 mL
2 tbsp.	finely chopped candied ginger	30 mL
1 tbsp.	liquid honey	15 mL
1-2 tbsp.	unsweetened orange juice	15-30 mL
3 cups	sliced fresh peaches	750 mL
1 cup	fresh blueberries	250 mL
1 cup	quartered fresh strawberries	250 mL
1 cup	fresh raspberries	250 mL

Sauce: In a small bowl, combine yogurt, candied ginger, honey and orange juice. Stir well and set aside.

In a large glass bowl, gently stir peach slices and berries together. Pour sauce over and toss gently to combine. Serve immediately.

Serves 6-8

Raspberries contain phytonutrients that provide antioxidant, anti-cancer (inhibiting cancer cells and tumor formation) and antimicrobial protection. They are an excellent source of manganese and vitamin C, and a good source of riboflavin, folate, niacin, magnesium, potassium and copper. They are a very good fruit choice because of their minimal impact on blood sugars.

Watermelon Sorbet

The intense flavor of this icy watermelon sorbet is incredibly refreshing.

½ cup	water	125 mL
⅓ cup	sugar	75 mL
6 cups	watermelon, seeded, cubed	1.5 L
2 tbsp.	lemon juice	30 mL

Combine water and sugar in a saucepan; bring to a boil; cook and stir until sugar is dissolved. Cool. Place watermelon in a food processor or blender and process or blend until smooth. Combine sugar syrup, puréed watermelon and lemon juice. Pour into a 5 x 9" (13 x 23 cm) loaf pan; freeze until firm. Break frozen mixture into large pieces and place in a large bowl. With an electric mixer, beat at medium speed until mixture is smooth but not melted. Return mixture to loaf pan. Cover tightly; freeze until sorbet is firm, about 4-6 hours. To serve, scoop sorbet into dessert dishes; garnish as desired. Serve immediately.

Serves 4-6

Pictured on page 155.

Whipped Cream – A Lighter Version

1 cup	whipping cream	250 mL
2-3 tbsp.	icing (confectioner's) sugar	30-45 mL
1 tsp.	vanilla	5 mL
½-¾ cup	plain low-fat yogurt	125-175 mL

In a small bowl, with an electric mixer, beat cream until peaks begin to form. Add sugar and vanilla; continue beating until peaks hold when the beaters are lifted. Fold in yogurt.

Makes 2 cups (500 mL)

Variations: Substitute 2 tbsp. (30 mL) of your favorite liqueur, cognac or rum for the vanilla; OR substitute your favorite low-fat flavored yogurt for the plain yogurt.

Pineapple and Strawberry Sorbet

Sweet and luscious, this is the perfect summer dessert.

2 cups	halved fresh strawberries	500 mL
8 oz.	can unsweetened crushed pineapple with juice	250 mL
¼ cup	sugar	60 mL
1 tbsp.	lemon juice	15 mL
1 tbsp.	chopped fresh mint leaves	15 mL

In a food processor or blender, combine strawberries and pineapple with juice. Cover and process or blend until smooth. Add sugar, lemon juice and chopped mint; process until smooth. Pour purée into a 5 x 9" (13 x 23 cm) loaf pan. Cover; freeze for 4 hours or until firm. Break frozen mixture into small chunks and place chunks in a mixing bowl. With an electric mixer, beat at medium speed until mixture is smooth, but not melted. Return mixture to loaf pan. Cover tightly; freeze until sorbet is firm, about 4-6 hours. To serve, scoop sorbet into dessert dishes; garnish with fresh mint sprigs. Serve immediately.

Serves 4-6

Pineapple (fresh) is rich in bromelain which aids digestion and can effectively reduce swelling and inflammatory conditions such as sore throat, acute sinusitis, arthritis, gout and hastening recovery from surgery and wounds. For best effect, eat pineapple alone between meals. Pineapple is rich in vitamin C, which provides antioxidant protection and immune support, and is an excellent source of manganese and vitamin B_1, which help in energy production and antioxidant defense.

Sweet, juicy watermelon is actually packed with some of the most important antioxidants in nature. It is an excellent source of vitamin C and a very good source of vitamin A. Through its concentration of beta-carotene, watermelon is also rich in the B vitamins necessary for energy production. It is known to have an even greater abundance of lycopene than tomatoes.

Orange-Blueberry Frozen Yogurt

Creamy and full of flavor, absolutely delicious.

2	strips of orange zest	2
½ cup	sugar	125 mL
1 tsp.	unflavored gelatin	5 mL
½ cup	skim milk	125 mL
2 tbsp.	honey	30 mL
1½ cups	fresh blueberries, or frozen, thawed	375 mL
¼ cup	unsweetened orange juice	60 mL
1 cup	fat-free plain yogurt	250 mL

With a potato peeler, cut 2 strips of orange zest the full length of an orange; set aside. In a small saucepan, combine sugar and gelatin; stir in milk and strips of orange zest. Cook and stir over low heat until gelatin dissolves. Remove from heat; add honey. Cool. In a blender or food processor, combine blueberries and orange juice, blend or process until puréed and mixture is smooth. Remove orange zest from gelatin mixture and discard. In a metal bowl, combine berry purée, gelatin mixture and plain yogurt; mix well.

Refrigerator-Freezer Instructions: Be sure yogurt is in a METAL bowl. Cover with foil or plastic wrap and place in freezer compartment of refrigerator. Freeze for 2-3 hours, or until firm at the edges and semisoft in the center. Remove from freezer and, with an electric mixer, beat on medium-high speed until soft, but not melted. Repeat freezing and beating 1 or 2 more times to reach yogurt consistency. Store, covered, in freezer until serving time.

Makes 4 cups (1 L)

Blueberries are an antioxidant powerhouse. The rich blue-red pigments in blueberries improve the integrity of support structures in the veins and entire vascular system and may also protect against chronic diseases, including cancer. They protect the brain from oxidative stress and may help reduce the effects of age-related brain diseases. They act as astringents in the digestive system and also promote urinary tract health.

Peach Frozen Yogurt

Peaches and maple syrup make a creamy yogurt dessert.

3	large peaches, peeled and chopped	3
¼ cup	sugar	60 mL
1 tsp.	unflavored gelatin	5 mL
½ cup	skim milk	125 mL
⅓ cup	maple syrup	75 mL
1 cup	fat-free plain yogurt	250 mL

In a blender or food processor, blend or process peaches and sugar until peaches are finely chopped but not puréed; transfer to a metal bowl. In a small saucepan, sprinkle gelatin over milk; let stand for 1 minute. Place over low heat and, stirring constantly, cook until gelatin dissolves; pour into peach mixture. Add maple syrup and yogurt to peach mixture and stir well. Freeze as per instructions on page 148.

Makes 4 cups (1 L)

Yogurt with live bacteria cultures is the best choice. It promotes a healthier immune response, increasing resistance to immune-related diseases and helping to prevent and heal arthritis and protect against ulcers. Yogurt is a very good source of calcium, phosphorus, vitamin B_2 and iodine, plus a good source of vitamin B_{12} and B_5, zinc, potassium, molybdenum and protein. One or two servings (1 cup/250 mL per serving) of yogurt per day can help significantly increase fat loss and minimize muscle loss. It also enhances breath freshness and promotes healthier teeth and gums. The calcium in yogurt also helps to build bones.

Cherry Berry Frozen Yogurt

The sweet flavor of cherries with a cranberry tang.

1 cup	cranberry juice cocktail	250 mL
1 tsp.	unflavored gelatin	5 mL
1 cup	pitted fresh sweet cherries, or frozen pitted sweet cherries, thawed	250 mL
⅔ cup	sugar	150 mL
1 cup	fat-free plain yogurt	250 mL

In a small saucepan, combine cranberry juice and gelatin; let stand for 1 minute. Place over low heat and cook, stirring constantly, until gelatin is dissolved. Remove from heat and pour into a metal bowl. In a blender or food processor, combine pitted cherries and sugar; blend or process until almost smooth. Combine with gelatin mixture in metal bowl. Stir in yogurt. Freeze as per instructions on page 148.

Makes 4 cups (1 L)

Coconut Pineapple Frozen Yogurt

A tropical delight – a frozen piña colada!

¾ cup	skim milk	175 mL
1 cup	fat-free plain yogurt	250 mL
1½ oz.	pkg. sugar-free instant vanilla pudding mix (4-serving size)	42.5 g
8 oz.	can unsweetened crushed pineapple with juice	250 mL
¼ cup	flaked coconut	60 mL

In a metal bowl, combine milk, yogurt and pudding mix. Whisk for about 1 minute, or until mixture is smooth. Stir pineapple, with its juice, and coconut into pudding mixture. Freeze as per instructions on page 148.

Makes 4 cups (1 L)

Angel Berry Dessert

This trifle-style dessert is light and delicious. The tantalizing flavors of bananas and strawberries are a perfect ending to any meal.

2	medium-firm bananas, sliced	2
1	prepared angel food cake, cut into 1" (2.5 cm) cubes	1
2 cups	halved strawberries	500 mL
2 x ⅓ oz.	pkgs. sugar-free strawberry gelatin (4-serving size)	2 x 10 g
2 cups	boiling water	500 mL
1½ cups	cold water	375 mL
2-4 cups	whipped cream, page 146	500 mL-1 L

In a lightly buttered 9 x 13" (23 x 33 cm) baking pan, layer banana slices and cake cubes. Place strawberries over cake and press down gently. In a bowl, dissolve gelatin in boiling water; stir in cold water. Pour over strawberries. Refrigerate for 3-4 hours, or until set. Frost with whipped cream, less or more as you prefer.

Serves 12-14

Bananas are a good fiber source which, combined with three natural sugars, produces a sustained, substantial energy boost. They are low-fat, cholesterol and sodium free, and a rich source of vitamin B$_6$, potassium and magnesium, and a good source of vitamin C and iron. The potassium helps reduce the risk of high blood pressure and stroke (cardiovascular protection), improves alertness (brain power). Bananas have a natural antacid effect (ulcer protection), improve elimination, and the B vitamins help calm the nervous system.

Frozen Chocolate Cherry Yogurt Cake

A wonderful frozen "Black Forest" dessert that is sure to please everyone.

Chocolate Crust:

2 tbsp.	melted butter OR margarine	30 mL
2 tbsp.	corn syrup	30 mL
1 tbsp.	water	15 mL
1½ cups	chocolate wafer crumbs	375 mL

Yogurt Filling:

5 cups	frozen low-fat chocolate yogurt, slightly softened	1.25 L
19 oz.	can pitted dark cherries, drained, reserving juice	540 mL

Cherry Sauce:

19 oz.	can pitted dark cherries, drained, reserving juice	540 mL
2 cups	reserved cherry juice	500 mL
	water	
2 tbsp.	cornstarch	30 mL
¼ cup	sugar	
¼ cup	brandy OR rum	

Crust: Preheat oven to 350°F (180°C). In a small bowl, combine butter, corn syrup and water; add chocolate crumbs and mix well. Press into bottom of a 10" (25 cm) springform pan. Bake for 10-12 minutes. Remove from oven; let cool; freeze for 10 minutes, or until firm.

Filling: Coarsely chop cherries. In a large bowl, combine cherries with yogurt. Press onto prepared crust; smooth with spatula. Cover and freeze for 30-45 minutes, or until firm. Cake can be prepared to this point and frozen for up to 1 week.

Sauce: In a 2-cup (500 mL) measure, combine drained cherry juice and enough water to make 2 cups (500 mL). Combine cornstarch and sugar in a large heavy saucepan; stir in cherry juice. Place over medium heat; cook, stirring constantly, for about 2-4 minutes, or until thickened and clear. Remove from heat; stir in cherries and brandy.

Frozen Chocolate Cherry Yogurt Cake Continued

Simmer over low heat for 5 minutes. Serve warm. Sauce can be made ahead, cooled, then refrigerated. Reheat before serving.

To serve, pour cherry sauce over individual slices of frozen cake just before serving. Serve sauce separately in a pitcher at the table.

Serves 8

Variations: Substitute any flavors of frozen yogurt or use ice cream. Sauce may be made with canned or fresh peaches, apricots, etc. Use a complementary flavor of juice and yogurt or ice cream.

Peach Trifle

When peaches are in season, this is a definite must. The orange and peach flavors create a superbly delicious dessert.

1½ lbs.	fresh peaches, pared and sliced	375 mL
1	prepared angel food cake, cut into 1" (2.5 cm) cubes	1
2 x ⅓ oz.	pkgs. sugar-free orange gelatin powders, prepared as package directions	2 x 10 g
1½ oz.	pkg. sugar-free instant vanilla pudding mix, prepared as package directions	42 g
2 cups	whipped cream, page 146	500 mL
¼ cup	toasted slivered almonds	60 mL

In a 9 x 13" (23 x 33 cm) baking pan, arrange half of the peach slices on the bottom of the pan; sprinkle angel food cake cubes over. Pour prepared gelatin over all; pressing down slightly to ensure all cake cubes are immersed. Refrigerate until set, then pour prepared pudding mix over gelatin layer, spreading evenly with back of spoon. Layer the remaining peach slices on top. Spread whipped cream over all; sprinkle with toasted almonds. Refrigerate to chill thoroughly, about 2-3 hours.

Serves 10-12

Mixed Fruit Pavlova

Pavlova is a huge favorite amongst Australians. It was created to celebrate the visit of Russian ballerina Anna Pavlova in the early 1900s. Our version of this meringue cake topped with cream and fresh fruit has considerably fewer calories.

Meringue Shell:

3	egg whites	3
¼ tsp.	cream of tartar	60 mL
⅔ cup	sugar	150 mL
1 tbsp.	cornstarch	15 mL

Fruit Filling:

2 cups	whipped cream, page 146, OR fruit sorbet OR ice cream	500 mL
3-4 cups	assorted sliced fresh seasonal fruit and/or berries	750 mL-1 L

Shell: Preheat oven to 250°F (120°C). In a large glass or metal bowl, with an electric mixer, beat egg whites with cream of tartar until soft peaks form. Gradually beat in sugar, 1 tbsp. (15 mL) at a time, until glossy peaks form. Blend in cornstarch. Line a baking sheet with lightly buttered foil; spread with meringue to make a 9" (23 cm) circle forming 1" (2.5 cm) high rounded rim. Bake for 1-1½ hours, or until crisp. Turn oven off and let meringue stand in oven for 8-12 hours. Remove from oven and gently peel off foil; place on a serving plate.

Spoon whipped cream into meringue shell. In a large bowl, mix fresh fruit and/or berries together and arrange on top of whipped cream. To serve, cut with a serrated knife.

Serves 8-10

Variation: *Strawberries in Chocolate Pavlova*: Make meringue as for Pavlova; fold in 2 oz. (55 g) of finely chopped semisweet chocolate at the end. Bake as Pavlova shell. Spoon 2 cups (500 mL) whipped cream, page 146, into shell. Arrange 3 cups (750 mL) quartered strawberries over cream.

Pictured opposite.

Desserts

Mixed Fruit Pavlova, page 154
Watermelon Sorbet, page 146

Heavenly Light Lemon Pie

Truly divine – this crisp meringue shell is filled with a lovely tart lemon curd.

1	Pavlova meringue shell, see page 154	1

Lemon Filling:

2 tbsp.	cornstarch	30 mL
1½ tbsp.	all-purpose flour	22 mL
¾ cup	sugar	175 mL
⅛ tsp.	salt	0.5 mL
1 cup	water	250 mL
2	egg yolks, slightly beaten	2
1 tbsp.	grated lemon zest	15 mL
¼ cup	lemon juice	60 mL
1 tsp.	butter OR margarine	5 mL
1-2 cups	whipped cream, page 146	250-500 mL

Prepare meringue shell.

Filling: In a small saucepan, combine cornstarch, flour, sugar and salt. Gradually add water, stirring until smooth. Place saucepan over medium heat and bring to a boil; cook for 1 minute. Remove from heat. Quickly stir some of hot mixture into egg yolks. Return all to hot mixture; stir to blend. Return to heat; cook over low heat until thickened, about 5 minutes, stirring constantly. Remove from heat; stir in lemon zest, lemon juice and butter. Allow to cool completely. Pour into meringue shell; top with whipped cream. To serve, cut with a serrated knife.

Serves 8-10

Variation: Top with blueberries or raspberries or sliced strawberries.

Pineapple Banana Cheesecake

A light, no-cook dessert, the pineapple and banana combination gives this a taste of the tropics.

½ cup	crushed granola	125 mL
2 tbsp.	unflavored gelatin (2 x 7 g env.)	30 mL
½ cup	cold water	125 mL
½ cup	boiling water	125 mL
19 oz.	can unsweetened crushed pineapple with juice	540 mL
1⅓ cups	dry skim milk powder	325 mL
3 tsp.	vanilla	15 mL
3 tsp.	unsweetened orange juice concentrate	15 mL
1	ripe banana	1
2 tsp.	grated orange zest	10 mL
	strawberries for garnish	

Sprinkle granola crumbs in a 9" (23 cm) pie plate. In a small bowl, sprinkle gelatin over cold water. Allow to sit for 2 minutes. Add boiling water and stir until gelatin is completely dissolved. In a blender or food processor, combine gelatin mixture, pineapple with juice, milk powder, vanilla, orange juice concentrate and banana. Process until smooth and fluffy and well blended. Stir in the grated orange zest; pour over granola crumbs in pie plate. Chill until firm, 6-8 hours or overnight. Garnish with strawberries.

Serves 8-10

Lemon Delight Cheesecake

A delicious, creamy cheesecake with just a slight hint of lemon.

1 tbsp.	graham cracker crumbs	15 mL
1 cup	low-fat cottage cheese	250 mL
2 x 8 oz.	light cream cheese, softened	2 x 250 g
⅔ cup	sugar	150 mL
2 tbsp.	all-purpose flour	30 mL
3	eggs	3
2 tbsp.	skim milk	30 mL
2 tsp.	grated lemon zest	10 mL
1 tsp.	lemon juice	5 mL
½ tsp.	vanilla extract	2 mL
	fresh berries for garnish	

Preheat oven to 325°F (160°C). Lightly butter the bottom of a 9" (23 cm) springform pan. Sprinkle with graham crumbs; press lightly. Place cottage cheese in a blender or food processor; blend or process until smooth; transfer to a large bowl. With an electric mixer, at medium speed, beat cottage cheese, cream cheese, sugar and flour until well blended. Add eggs, 1 at a time, beating well after each addition. Beat in milk, lemon zest, lemon juice and vanilla. Pour into prepared pan. Bake for 45-50 minutes, or until center is almost set. Remove from oven; loosen cake from pan rim. Cool completely before removing pan rim. Garnish with raspberries, strawberries or blueberries.

Serves 10-12

Orange Cheesecake with Strawberry Glaze

Elegant and showy. This light, creamy orange cheesecake is complemented with strawberries in an orange-flavored glaze. For a special occasion, replace orange juice with Grand Marnier in the glaze ingredients.

Graham Crust:

1 cup	graham cracker crumbs	250 mL
1 tbsp.	butter OR margarine, melted	15 mL
2 tbsp.	corn syrup	30 mL

Orange Cheesecake:

1 cup	sugar	250 mL
2 tbsp.	grated orange zest	30 mL
½ cup	unsweetened orange juice	125 mL
2 cups	low-fat cottage cheese	500 mL
1 cup	low-fat plain yogurt, drained	250 mL
8 oz.	light cream cheese, cubed and softened	250 g
2	eggs	2
3	egg whites	3
¼ cup	flour	60 mL
1 tsp.	vanilla	5 mL

Strawberry Glaze:

15 oz.	pkg. frozen sliced strawberries in syrup, thawed	425 mL
4 tsp.	cornstarch	20 mL
4 tsp.	unsweetened orange juice	20 mL

Crust: Preheat oven to 350°F (180°C). Centre a 10" (25 cm) springform pan on a large square of foil. Press foil to pan sides to keep out water when baking filling. In a small bowl, combine graham crumbs, melted butter and corn syrup. Mix well and press evenly over bottom of pan. Bake for 10 minutes. Remove from oven and set aside.

Orange Cheesecake with Strawberry Glaze Continued

Cheesecake: Preheat oven to 325°F (160°C). In a food processor, combine sugar, orange zest, orange juice and cottage cheese. Process for about 30 seconds, or until well blended and no longer granular. With motor running, add yogurt and cream cheese; blend until combined. Add eggs, egg whites, flour and vanilla; process until smooth, about 30-40 seconds. Pour batter over prepared crust.

Set springform pan in a larger pan and pour in enough hot water to come 1" (2.5 cm) up sides of pan. Bake for 1¼-1½ hours, or until set around the edges but still jiggly in the center. Turn oven off; quickly run a knife around the edge of the cake and let stand in oven for 1 hour. Remove from larger pan and transfer to a rack. Remove foil and let cool completely. Cover and refrigerate for at least 8 hours or up to 2 days.

Strawberry Glaze: In a small saucepan, whisk together strawberries with syrup and cornstarch until smooth. Bring to a boil over medium heat, stirring constantly; cook and stir for about 1 minute, or until thickened and clear. Remove from heat and stir in orange juice. Allow to cool.

Remove cake from pan. Pour strawberry glaze evenly over cheesecake. Refrigerate for at least 2-4 hours before serving. If desired, Strawberry Glaze can be served separately in a serving pitcher at the table.

Serves 12

Variation: For a chocolate crust, substitute chocolate wafer crumbs for the graham cracker crumbs.

My Favorite Creamy Rice Pudding

Create your own healthier rice pudding – here are the basics and lots of delicious options. For creamier pudding, use short-grain or medium rice.

Stove-Top Rice Pudding

1½ cups	cooked rice (white – long, short OR medium grain, jasmine OR basmati, OR brown)	375 mL
2 cups	milk, divided (use skim, 1%, 2%, whole OR evaporated skim milk)	500 mL
⅔ cup	raisins	150 mL
⅓ cup	sugar	75 mL
¼ tsp.	salt	1 mL
1	egg, beaten	1
sprinkle	EACH cinnamon and nutmeg	sprinkle
½ tsp.	vanilla	2 mL

In a large heavy saucepan, combine rice, 1½ cups (375 mL) milk, raisins, sugar and salt. Cook, covered, for 15-20 minutes, until thick and creamy. Beat egg with remaining ½ cup (125 mL) milk and slowly stir into rice mixture with cinnamon and nutmeg. Cook 2 minutes more, stirring constantly. Remove from heat and stir in vanilla. Serve warm or cold. See serving suggestions under Variations on the next page.

Serves 4-6

Variations:

Cooking times will vary for different types of rice, follow package directions. Skim milk makes a very good creamy pudding. Use skim, 1%, 2% or whole milk, as you prefer.

Maple Rice Pudding: Use ½ cup (125 mL) maple syrup, or more to taste, to replace the sugar.

Lemon Rice Pudding: Add ½ tsp. (2 mL) grated lemon zest and 1-2 tsp. (5-10 mL) lemon juice.

Variations continued:

Use dark or golden raisins OR use all or part dried cranberries OR blueberries OR chopped dried apricots.

Add ¼ cup (60 mL) toasted almonds – stir in with vanilla.

Substitute soy OR almond milk for milk.

Replace half or all of white sugar with brown sugar.

Replace sugar with Splenda.

For a creamier texture, add more milk.

Plump raisins in rum or brandy before adding to pudding.

Top rice pudding with maple syrup or plain yogurt.

Baked Rice Pudding

Make this creamy pudding with any of the variations suggested above.

1 cup	short-grain rice	250 mL
½ tsp.	salt	2 mL
¾ cup	sugar	175 mL
2 tsp.	vanilla	10 mL
7-8 cups	milk (more milk means a creamier pudding)	1.5 L
½ cup	raisins	125 mL
sprinkle	EACH nutmeg and cinnamon	sprinkle

Combine all ingredients in a buttered 2½-quart (2.5 L) ovenproof casserole. Bake, covered, at 275°F (130°C) for 3 hours, stirring occasionally. Remove cover for the last 30 minutes.

Serves 6-8

Four-Fruit Crisp

Juicy apples, pears, cranberries and raisins make this the best fruit crisp ever.

5 cups	apples, peeled and sliced	5
1 cup	dried cranberries	250 mL
1 cup	raisins, washed and dried	250 mL
5 cups	pears, peeled and sliced	1.25 L
½ cup	apple juice	125 mL
1 tsp.	grated lemon zest	5 mL
2 tbsp.	lemon juice	30 mL
2 tsp.	ground nutmeg	10 mL

Crunchy Almond Oat Topping:

¾ cup	all-purpose flour	175 mL
½ cup	brown sugar	125 mL
½ cup	butter OR margarine	125 mL
½ cup	slivered almonds	125 mL
½ cup	rolled oats	125 mL

Preheat oven to 350°F (180°C). In a 9 x 13" (23 x 33 cm) baking dish, layer apples, cranberries, raisins, then pears. In a small bowl, stir together apple juice, lemon zest, lemon juice and nutmeg; drizzle over fruit.

Topping: In a large bowl, combine flour and sugar. With a pastry blender or 2 knives, cut in butter until crumbly. Stir in almonds and rolled oats; sprinkle evenly over fruit. Bake for 50-60 minutes, or until crisp and golden and fruit is tender and bubbling. Let cool slightly. May be served warm or cold, with or without frozen vanilla yogurt, ice cream or whipped cream.

Serves 10-12

Variations: Substitute peaches and blueberries for the apples and pears.

Baked Apples with a Hint of Ginger

A different way to have your fruit and cookies. Delicious served with plain or frozen yogurt or ice cream.

½ cup	gingersnap cookie crumbs (6-8 small cookies)	125 mL
2 tbsp.	butter OR margarine, melted	30 mL
3 tbsp.	shredded coconut OR chopped pecans	45 mL
2 tbsp.	dried cranberries	30 mL
¼ tsp.	ground nutmeg	1 mL
2	apples	2
¼ cup	water	60 mL

Preheat oven to 350°F (180°C). In a food processor or blender, process gingersnap cookies until coarse crumbs form; set aside. In a small bowl, melt butter in microwave. Stir in cookie crumbs, coconut, cranberries and nutmeg. Slice apples in half crosswise. Scoop out and discard core, along with enough apple flesh to create a hollow that will hold about 2 tbsp. (30 mL) crumb mixture. Place apples in a 9" (23 cm) pie plate, skin side down. Spoon crumb mixture into apple hollows and press down lightly. Mound remaining mixture into centers. Pour water into bottom of pie plate. Cover with foil; bake for 30 minutes. Uncover and bake until apples are very tender but still hold their shape, an additional 15-20 minutes.

Serves 2

Variation: For **Baked Ginger Pears**, substitute pears for apples and bake as above, checking to see if done after an additional 10 minutes.

Raisins, Cranberries and Apricots in Baked Apples

These are colorful and full of flavor.

4 large	baking apples (Rome Beauty, Braeburn, Golden Delicious, Granny Smith, Gala, Gravenstein, York Imperial)	4 large
½ cup	golden raisins	125 mL
½ cup	dried cranberries	125 mL
⅓ cup	Demerara sugar, packed	75 mL
¼ cup	chopped dried apricots	60 mL
¾ tsp.	ground cinnamon OR allspice	3 mL
3-4 tbsp.	butter, melted	45-60 mL
2 cups	sparkling apple-cranberry juice	800 mL
¼ cup	frozen concentrated cranberry juice cocktail, thawed	60 mL

Preheat oven to 400°F (200°C). Remove stems from apples. Using melon baller, scoop out core of each apple, making 1" (2.5 cm) wide hollow center, leaving bottom of apple intact. Make ⅛" (3 mm) deep cut in skin around center of each apple. Arrange apples, hollowed side up, in 8" (20 cm) square glass baking pan. Mix raisins, cranberries, sugar, apricots and ½ tsp. (2 mL) cinnamon in a small bowl. Pack fruit mixture into hollows in apples. Sprinkle remaining fruit mixture around apples in pan. Drizzle butter into filling and around apples in pan. Pour sparkling juice and cranberry concentrate into pan. Sprinkle remaining ¼ tsp. (1 mL) cinnamon over apples. Bake apples, uncovered, until tender, basting occasionally with pan juices, about 1 hour 10 minutes.

Transfer apples to 4 bowls. Pour pan juices into a medium saucepan and boil until thick enough to coat spoon, about 4 minutes. Spoon sauce over apples.

Serves 4

Variation: For **Baked Pears with Raisins, Cranberries and Apricots**, substitute pears for apples and bake as above, checking to see if done after 50 minutes.

Oatmeal Chocolate Chip Cookies

Oatmeal chocolate chip cookies like mom used to make – these are great when you need a chocolate fix.

4 tbsp.	butter OR margarine	60 mL
⅔ cup	brown sugar	150 mL
½ cup	sugar	125 mL
1	egg	1
2 tsp.	vanilla	10 mL
⅓ cup	light sour cream	75 mL
1 cup	all-purpose flour	250 mL
½ tsp.	baking soda	2 mL
½ tsp.	salt	2 mL
1 cup	rolled oats	250 mL
¾ cup	semisweet chocolate chips	175 mL
½ cup	chopped walnuts	125 mL

Preheat oven to 375°F (190°C). In a large bowl, cream butter and sugars together with an electric mixer at high speed until light and fluffy, about 45-60 seconds. Add egg and vanilla; beat until light yellow and creamy, about 2 minutes. Stir in sour cream with a wooden spoon. In a small bowl, combine flour, baking soda, salt and rolled oats. Stir into butter mixture all at once, mixing only until ingredients are well combined. Do not over mix or cookies may become tough. Stir in chocolate chips and walnuts. Drop dough by heaping teaspoonfuls (7 mL) onto lightly buttered baking sheets. Bake for 10-12 minutes. Remove from oven and allow cookies to cool on baking sheets for 2 minutes, then transfer to wire racks to cool completely. Store in an airtight container for up to 2 weeks, or wrap well and freeze for up to 3 months.

Makes 36 cookies

Note: Using sour cream provides that "melt in your mouth" texture and allows us to significantly cut the fat content.

Index

Share A Taste of Healthier Choices

Order at $14.95 per book plus $3.50 (total order) for postage and handling.

A Taste of Brunch – number of books _____ x $14.95 = $ _____

A Taste of Christmas – number of books _____ x $14.95 = $ _____

A Taste of the Great Outdoors – number of books ____ x $14.95 = $ _____

A Taste of Healthier Choices – number of books _____ x $14.95 = $ _____

Shipping and handling charge _____ = $ _3.50_

Subtotal _____ = $ _____

In Canada add 7% GST _____(Subtotal x .07) = $ _____

Total enclosed_____ = $ _____

U.S. and international orders payable in U.S. funds / Price is subject to change.

NAME: _____

STREET: _____

CITY: _____   PROV./STATE _____

COUNTRY _____   POSTAL CODE/ZIP_____

Please make cheque or money order payable to:

Three Sisters Publishing Inc.   **www.3sistersbooks.com**
12234 – 49 Street
Edmonton, Alberta, Canada   T5W 3A8

For fund raising or volume purchase prices,
contact **Three Sisters Publishing**.

Please allow 2-3 weeks for delivery.

Other books available from Three Sisters Publishing Inc.

For best results, share the good food in all of these books with good friends.

A Taste of Brunch

by Jacquie Schmit, Eileen Mandryk, Jo Wuth

Beautiful brunches – treat yourself and your family, enjoy your own parties with this superb collection of easy-make recipes. Casual or elegant; cottage, garden, deck or townhouse, these brunch menus and recipes offer great flexibility year-round.

ISBN 1-895292-85-9

A Taste of Christmas – A Treasury of Holiday Recipes, Menus, Customs, Crafts and Gift-Giving Ideas

by Jacquie Schmit, Eileen Mandryk, Jo Wuth

Enhance the magic of Christmas with the tantalizing aromas of Christmas baking and heartwarming gifts of homemade delicacies. Tempting recipes, suggestions for easy preparation. Menus for the whole holiday season.

ISBN 1-895292-85-9

A Taste of the Great Outdoors – Cooking on the Go for RVs, Motor Coaches, Camping & Picnics

by Jacquie Schmit, Eileen Mandryk, Jo Wuth

Escape from the everyday – enjoy terrific food with minimum time, effort, ingredients and maximum flavor. Includes tips for easier, faster food preparation. More time for you, less time in the kitchen, savor the freedom of the great outdoors.

ISBN 1-894022-33-5

All books are: $14.95 retail; 172 pages; 8 colour photographs; perfect bound